U and I

Nicholson Baker was born in 1957. He has written four novels, *Room Temperature*, *The Mezzanine*, *Vox* and *The Fermata*. He is also the author of a book of essays, *The Size of Thoughts*. He lives in California.

D0524149

NICHOLSON BAKER

U and I

A True Story

Granta Books
London

Granta Publications, 2/3 Hanover Yard, London N1 8BE

First published in Great Britain by Granta Books 1991
This edition published by Granta Books 1998

A CIP catalogue record for this book is available
from the British Library.

3 5 7 9 10 8 6 4 2

Printed and bound in Great Britain
by Mackays of Chatham PLC

FOR MY MOTHER

It may be *us* they wish to meet but it's themselves they want to talk about.

CYRIL CONNOLLY

U and I

I

On August 6, 1989, a Sunday, I lay back as usual with my feet up in a reclining aluminum deck chair padded with blood-dotted pillows in my father-in-law's study in Berkeley (we were house-sitting) and arranged my keyboard, resting on an abridged dictionary, on my lap. I began to type the date and the time, 9:46 A.M. I had no idea what subject I was going to cover that morning. A week or so earlier I had finished and sent off a novel, my second, and I was still full of the misleading momentum that, while it makes the completion of novels possible, also generally imparts a disappointingly thin and rushed feeling to their second halves or final thirds, as the writer's growing certainty that he is finally a pro, finally getting the hang of it, coincides exactly with that unpleasant fidgety sensation on the reader's part that he is locked into a set of characters and surroundings he knows a bit too well by now to enjoy. I wanted very much to keep slapping esemplastically away at the keys, and the imminence of this very pleasure made the words "the act of beginning to write in the morning never loses its pleasure" appear in the to-be-typed lounge in my awareness; but before I could move my fingers, I recalled that Updike had said something similar in *Self-Consciousness*: "In the morning light one can write breezily, without the slightest acceleration of one's pulse, about what one cannot contemplate in the dark without turning in panic to God." A memorable sentence for me (though I only remembered the first half) not only because it seemed simple and true, but because I had read it twice, first quoted in a book review and then in the book itself. And with this memory of Updike I hesitated; I didn't type what I was going to type; I shifted course.

Donald Barthelme had just died, on July 23. My wife had seen the Associated Press obituary in the newspaper. My sense of being detached from the literary and academic communities, if there are such things, was reinforced by having learned of his death not through some grief-stricken phone call from a close associate or a devoted student of Barthelme's, but merely from the local paper, whose information is available to all. I stared distractedly for half an hour, unsure of what to do, while my wife stood in the middle of the rug with round eyes, saying, "I'm so sorry, I'm so sorry." I decided I should write a letter of condolence to his editor at *The New Yorker*, but I didn't begin it. Then my daughter got an ear infection. On the first of August she said, "I'm going to choke, Daddy, I don't want to choke," and I held her awkwardly over the kitchen sink, cupping her forehead in my palm (suddenly remembering, from when my mother had held my own forehead, how this brain-embrace transferred some of the misery of your sickness to a higher power), and I felt her stomach muscles powerfully tighten. I took her to the doctor that day and got her some antibiotics and when we returned I remembered that I owed my great-uncle Dick, who was very ill, a letter. Instead of writing it I made several attempts at the letter to *The New Yorker* about Barthelme. I rejected "I'm torn up by," "heart-broken," and "He was a master." But as I struggled to formulate something that sounded unmannered, I noticed that there was a morally bothersome taint to the effort I was making. *Those black bars, those black bars*, I kept thinking, that *The New Yorker* tastefully puts over its obituaries: the eulogies always come at the very end of an issue, and lately there had been ones for Saxon and Addams. But the one uppermost in my mind was the one that Updike wrote after Nabokov died, reprinted in *Hugging the Shore*: I remembered no particular phrase from it, except one smoothly saying that the consensus would probably be that *Lolita* was his best novel in English, and *The Gift* his best in Russian (this judgment stayed with me because these two weren't my own favorites), but I did remember its tone: gentle, serious, unmaudlin, fluent without affectation, deliberately unspectacular and unrivalrous—a model obituary. And I knew that Barthelme's editor at *The New Yorker* was likely to write the Barthelme obituary, and that the tribute would probably include anonymous quotations from associates and fellow writers. *Here* precisely was the detectable taint of wrongdoing in my attitude, for some not insubstantial fraction of what was prodding me to write the letter of condolence was my self-centered, ungrieving ambition to come up with at least one sentence in it that would be in the same league as many in Updike's obituary for Nabokov, and which would as a result have the sad but not-choked-up quotability that would allow me anonymously to "make" the Barthelme obituary, as if I were making some team.

Disgusted with my mixed motives, I wrote in reaction a terse, four-sentence, utterly unexcerptable note that essentially said: miss him, wonderful titles, effortless originality, thank you publishing him, greats of this century. "It's kind of choppy," my wife decided. I sent it anyway; the choppiness was evidence of my virtue. (The obituary came out in due time; not, as it turned out, with a black bar above it at the back of the magazine, but as a "Notes and Comment" in the front, and there were indeed several quotations in it—none from me.) But I was still sad. My reaction, attractively self-denying though it was, didn't meet the gravity of the case. I thought very briefly of writing a neo-Jamesian story about a guy who hears of the death of a big-name writer he has long admired and who agonizes over the letter of condolence to the big name's editor, reproaches himself for having to agonize rather than simply and spontaneously to grieve, worries about whether he should destroy his early drafts of the letter, which betray how hard he worked to hit the proper spontaneous note, or whether such a compounding of deceptions, by robbing biographers of this material, furnished brave proof of how lightly he took his literary prospects. But a fictionalization was, so I thought, a far more crudely opportunist use of my bewilderment at Barthelme's death than a lushly quotable letter would have been.

I also considered the prospect of writing the critical appreciation of Barthelme that I'd had in mind for several years. It was, after all, the standard way to fill the hole a writer leaves behind. Henry James, for instance, wrote big lovely commemorative things on Emerson and Hawthorne after they were gone; he panned Trollope harshly while Trollope was alive to read the review, but the minute Trollope dozed to his final rest, James wrote of him full of immense tolerant affection. And Updike, too, wrote big lovely things on Hawthorne and Melville, and major reviews of Wilson's posthumous diaries, as well as the Nabokov obituary. So, inspired by these advanced practitioners, I might reread Barthelme slowly and carefully, working myself up (as I knew from college I tended to do with any intrinsically good writer to whom I devoted lots of time) into an awestruck, fanatical receptivity to his proprietary strengths, and excusing his weaknesses in a way that made me seem wise and clear-sighted, rather than merely blind. But why bother? Barthelme would never know. And in any case, I wanted my choice of what to read at a given moment to be the outcome of more multiply confluent causes than the simple requirement of an obituarizing overview. That is, I wanted to reread Barthelme only when I really wanted to reread Barthelme, and not when his death suddenly obliged me to do so. He had died somewhat out of fashion, too, and I was curious to watch firsthand the microbiologies of upward revaluation or of progressive obscurity, as I had failed to observe them in the earlier cases of, say, John O'Hara or John Gardner. I felt no particular eagerness yet to try to make my personal opinion, to the extent that I could really be said to have something as fixed as an opinion about him, prevail.

That phrase which reviewers take such pains to include when delivering their judgments—when they say that *among living writers* so-and-so is or isn't of the first rank—had once seemed to me unnecessary: the writing, I had thought, was good or bad, no matter whether the writer was here or not. But now, after the news of Barthelme's death, this simple fact of *presence or absence*, which I had begun to recognize in a small way already, now became the single most important supplemental piece of information I felt I could know about a writer: more important than his age when he wrote a particular work, or his nationality, his sex (forgive the pronoun), political leanings, even whether he did or did not have, in someone's opinion, any talent. *Is he alive or dead?*— just tell me that. The intellectual surface we offer to the dead has undergone a subtle change of texture and chemistry; a thousand particulars of delight and fellow-feeling and forbearance begin reformulating themselves the moment they cross the bar. The living are always potentially thinking about and doing just what we are doing: being pulled through a touchless car wash, watching a pony chew a carrot, noticing that orange scaffolding has gone up around some prominent church. The conclusions they draw we know to be conclusions drawn from how things are now. Indeed, for me, as a beginning novelist, all other living writers form a control group for whom the world is a placebo. The dead can be helpful, needless to say, but we can only guess sloppily about how they would react to this emergent particle of time, which is all the time we have. And when we do guess, we are unfair to them. Even when, as with Barthelme, the dead have died unexpectedly and relatively young, we give them their moment of solemnity and then quickly begin patronizing them biographically, talking about how they "delighted in" x or "poked fun at" at y—phrases that by their very singsong cuteness betray how alien and childlike the shades now are to us. Posthumously their motives become ludicrously simple, their delights primitive and unvarying: all their emotions wear stage makeup, and we almost never flip their books across the room out of impatience with something they've said. We can't really understand them anymore. Readers of the living are always, whether they know it or not, to some degree seeing the work through the living writer's own eyes; feeling for him when he flubs, folding into their reactions to his early work constant subauditional speculations as to whether the writer himself would at this moment wince or nod with approval at some passage in it. But the dead can't suffer embarrassment by some admission or mistake they have made. We sense this imperviousness and adjust our sympathies accordingly.

Yet in other ways the dead gain by death. The level of autobiographical fidelity in their work is somehow less important, or, rather, extreme fidelity does not seem to harm, as it does with the living, our appreciation for the work. The living are "just" writing about their own lives; the dead are writing about their irretrievable *lives*, wow wow wow. Egotism, monomania, the delusional traits of Blake or Smart or that guy who painted the electrically schizophrenic cats are all engaging qualities in the dead. To show our sophistication across time, we laugh politely whenever we sense, say in Sheridan, that a dead person is trying to be funny, although seldom with the real honking abandonment that the living can inspire. At one point in Boswell's *Life of Johnson*, the subject of Garrick's recent funeral comes up. They talk about how grand and extravagant it was. A woman says that *she* heard that there were six horses drawing each coach in the procession. Here Johnson finally loses his patience and says, "Madam, there were no more six horses than six phoenixes." When I first read this, Johnson's lovable huffiness seemed funny enough to merit a shout and a thigh slap; but right on the tail of this response I was confused, because at the moment I laughed I had been sure in the genuineness of my amusement that Johnson had to be alive somewhere, right then, in seclusion, forgotten by reporters, in order for his words to have made so direct a connection with me. And then the certainty faded, and I heard the hollow droning dirge sound that you can make by humming or lowing through a mailing tube as I realized that no, Johnson was truly dead, and any comic life he had was of a mystical, phoenix-like impermanence—and now I know, looking at his sentence again, that one part of what made it seem funny to me was that such indignation is more comic in dead men than in living men. You had not to be there.

So I abandoned Barthelme completely. But the various morbidities his death occasioned—as well as the sense of fragility and preciousness of all life that is inevitably triggered by even a minor sickness in one's own child—were all close at hand when, on that Sunday morning early in August, I hesitated for an instant after being reminded of

Updike's sentence about how easily the words come in the morning. Updike was much more important to me than Barthelme as a model and influence, and now the simple knowledge that he was alive and writing and had just published one of his best books, *Self-Consciousness*, felt like a piece of huge luck. How fortunate I was to be alive when he was alive! But though the book was very good—true to the way memory files things away under subject headings, and quite original, I thought, in building an autobiography out of discrete topical essays (as Harold Nicolson had made a sort of autobiography out of the fictionalized acquaintances in *Some People*)—Updike's book was uncomfortably full of notions of closure, the long view, failing bodily systems, and a kind of distant fly-fishing retrospection quite different from the young writer's need to get rid of the topmost layers of his grade-school and high-school memories so that he can move on without their constant distraction. The framed photograph on the front cover (his best-looking cover by far) was clearly the same one as is described in detail early in *Of the Farm*—he was coming clean. Nor had I liked reading a recent story of his about a man in his sixties who was startled, every day when he walked to the mailbox, by the doves that suddenly flapped up at his approach. The image was terrific, but the implication, that Updike was putting his intelligence to work on his forgetfulness, on what new could be said about the loss of one's powers, was very disturbing. With Barthelme gone

I suddenly got a glimpse of how disassembled and undirected and simply bereft I would feel if I were to learn suddenly through the Associated Press of Updike's death. All I wanted, all I counted on, was Updike's immortality: his open-ended stream of books, reviews, even poems, and especially responses to pert queries from *Mademoiselle* and *The New York Times Book Review*. I thought I remembered his saying recently in *Esquire*, in response to a survey question about popular fiction, that "in college I read what they told me and was much the better for it." I wanted more of these monocellular living appearances. More awards-acceptance speeches! He was, I felt, the model of the twentieth-century American man of letters: for him to die would be for my generation's personal connection with literature to die, and for us all to be confronted at last with the terrifying unmediated enormity of the cast-concrete university library, whose antitheft gates go *click-click-click-click* as we leave, dry laughter at how few books we can carry home with us.

"I should," I typed that morning, "write some appreciation" of Updike. And "it has to be done while he is alive." As with Barthelme, the idea of such an essay wasn't an entirely new plan. Since embarking on the project, I have found in my piles of typing various earlier mentions of exercitations like this—"Make a whole book about my obsession with Updike," I typed in October 1988, and followed it with three pages of notes. On September 8, 1987, after reading a number of Updike's reviews of Wilson and Nabokov, I typed: "Lately I have thought again of writing an essay on Updike." But, I said,

> with people you feel this complicatedly about, you should wait until they are dead, because then the fact that they are lost to you—that they aren't potentially on the other end of any piece of print—makes you value them so much more and more truly. Now I would have crabby things to say. . . .

See, Barthelme's death changed my mind completely. It felt positively contemptible now to wait until a writer has died to exercise one's best powers on his work—such a delay indeed seemed to me post-Barthelme to go directly counter to one of the principal aims of the novel itself, which is to capture pieces of mental life as truly as possible, as they unfold, with all the surrounding forces of circumstance that bear on a blastula of understanding allowed to intrude to the extent that they give a more accurate picture. The commemorative essay that pops up in some periodical, full of sad-clown sorrowfulness the year following the novelist's death (as in Henry James's essays on Zola and Trollope, or his long review of the first biography of Emerson), is unworthy of the fine-tuned descriptive capacities of the practicing novelist: confronted for once by a character in life that he actually does have the possibility to understand, given the daily literary regimen and tastes he shares with his subject, he instead lazily waits for the fixity of the autopsy table before doing a likeness. A beginning novelist like me is charged with describing life now, not writing history; and the huge contribution that the books by a senior living writer make to his life requires in its importance some attempt at a novelistically inclusive response.

I knew now that I had a real deadline: I had to write about Updike while people could still conceivably sneer at him simply for being at the top of the heap, before any false valedictory grand-old-man reverence crept in, as it inevitably would. The literary world demanded some sort of foreign-ness as the price of its attention: failing geographical dis-tance, senile remoteness would do. But what it lost in this demand was the possibility for real self-knowledge; for you can never come up with truths of an acceptable resolution if what you select for study is estranged by time or language or background or by a physiognomy in its authoritative, slow-talking decline. I would study my feelings for Updike while he was still in that phase of intellectual neglect that omnipresence and best-selling popularity inspire.

I began that morning to put down phrases or scenes I remembered from Updike's writing, just as they occurred to me. The first one was

vast, dying sea

I put an asterisk in front of those items, like the couple spitting at each other in *Marry Me*, that were bad memories.

It was an odd sensation: a particular item would arrive about once every ten seconds, not without some eyes-closed searching, separated from its predecessor in the list by a mental blur similar to the fast camera pan that separated scenes in old Batman shows. It felt as though I could continue typing these discrete, often phrasal memories of Updike for days. Some of the others in the train were:

(2) Mom reading Too Far to Go in a hotel when we were visiting some family—maybe around the time she and Dad had decided on a divorce

(5) The Chateau Mouton Rotschild [*sic*] that the man gives the kid in Updike's first story

(6) 'The blue below is ultramarine. Sometimes the blue below is green.' Misquoted

(7) The Bulgarian Poetess, title—and some sense of her: pulled back hair, 'coiffed.'

(10) The ice cube in Rabbit, Run

(14) 'and the sad curve of time it subtends,' dedication in Problems

(16) *'Seems' or 'seemed'—constantly used word

(17) Leeches climbing up legs in some short story

(20) Divot the size of an undershirt, that made Mom laugh so hard that Sunday.

I had a list of about thirty-five of these by the time I had to stop writing that morning and drive with my family to the zoo. But I did nothing with it. Instead I wrote a review of a biography of Flann O'Brien and an essay on model airplanes: frivolity. In mid-October my great uncle Dick committed suicide, overwhelmed by various incurable afflictions. My grandmother said that she felt very alone now, with nobody to tell her family memories to who would respond with supplemental ones of his own; and she quoted Oliver Wendell Holmes: "the last leaf upon the tree." The letter from him that I now never had to answer (his very first to me) rested at the top of a prioritized (and why not use that word if it is handy?) pile of correspondence that I had been guiltily eyeing for months. In it he mentions that he has read something of mine with "his sighted eye," and closes with: "I don't ask forgiveness for my poor penmanship—merely an understanding of a less than easy task." My wife stood in the middle of a different rug (we were back home by this time, done house-sitting) with round eyes, saying, "I'm so sorry, I'm so sorry." Again, in reaction, I felt the luck of being Updike's contemporary, but I did nothing with it.

Finally, a week or so later, on October 24, 1989, I read this in Henry James's long essay on Emerson:

It was impossible to be more honoured and cherished, far and near, than he was during his long residence in Concord, or more looked upon as the principal gentleman in the place. This was conspicuous to the writer of these remarks on the occasion of the curious, sociable, cheerful public funeral made for him in 1883 by all the countryside, arriving, as for the last honours to the first citizen, in trains, in waggons, on foot, in multitudes. It was a popular manifestation, the most striking I have ever seen provoked by the death of a man of letters.

Immediately I tried to picture what sort of "popular manifestation" there would be at Updike's funeral. Would the frumpy gathering of professional scribes be swelled by the modern equivalents of countryfolk: that is, secretaries, books-on-tape commuters, subscribers to the Franklin Library, members of Quality Paperback Book Club? The notion of all those thoughtful, likable, furrowed, middlebrow brows lowered in sadness seemed momentarily strange, after all of Updike's lively and shocking and un-Emersonian writing about nakedness, fucking in piles of laundry, pubic hair like seaweed, dirty Polaroids, his next-door-neighbor's pussy, and the rest—but then it seemed absolutely right. Updike was the first to take the penile sensorium under the wing of elaborate metaphorical prose. Once the sensation of the interior of a vagina has been compared to a ballet slipper (if my memory doesn't distort that unlocatable simile) the sexual revolution is complete: just as Emerson made the Oversoul, the luminous timeless sphere of pure thought, available to the earnest lecture-going farm worker, so Updike made the reader's solitary paperback-inspired convulsion an untrashy, cultivated attainment. (I myself have never successfully masturbated to Updike's writing, though I have to certain remembered scenes in Iris Murdoch; but someone I know says that she achieved a number of quality orgasms from *Couples* when she first read it at age thirteen.) In grieving for Updike, the somber, predominantly female citizens would be grieving for their own youthful sexual pasts, whose hard-core cavortings were now insulated by wools and goose downs of period charm, vague remorse, fuzzy remembrance, spousal forgiveness, and an overall sense of imperfect attempts at cutting loose; they would be mourning the man who, by bringing a serious, Prousto-Nabokovian, morally sensitive, National-Book-Award-winning prose style to bear on the micromechanics of physical lovemaking, first licensed their own moans. But the concrete visual image of mourners in contemporary dress gathered around a real grave was too powerful and distasteful to contemplate for more than an instant; recoiling, I thought, *But if he dies, he won't know how I feel about him*, and was horrified. That night I wrote inside the back cover of the Henry James paperback I'd been reading, "Make Updike thing into long essay," and the next day, trembling, I called the editor of *The Atlantic* to propose it to him.

2

But the editor wasn't in and didn't call me back. A week went by, including Halloween. My sense of relief increased daily. The prospect of writing a commissioned article about Updike was very frightening; not as frightening as the prospect of his death, but almost—more frightening, that is, than the prospect of my own death. I had almost no idea what I was going to be able to say, only that I did have things to say. And Updike could react, feel affronted, demolish me, ignore me, litigate. A flashy literary trial had some fantasy appeal, except that I knew that I would burst into tears if cross-examined by any moderately skillful attorney. But it probably wouldn't come to that. The outriggers of Updike's admirably quilled eyebrows would alter their tangential angles under the subdermal bunch of a frown of momentary consideration, and the eyes that have flown low over so many thousands of miles of print would finish skimming once over my words, and then a reply—wise, sensible, mildly amused, with a single burst of irritation perhaps to demonstrate out of kindness to me that my contortions had indeed received his undivided attention (like the burst in Nabokov's reply to Updike's "stylish" paragraph of praise in *Tri-Quarterly*, where Nabokov thanked Updike for liking the sad prostitute in *Lolita*, but was infuriated that Updike thought that Ada was "in a dimension or two" Nabokov's own wife, Vera)—would wing its way to *The Atlantic*. Or, much, much worse, would *not* wing. Especially in planning to talk about my premature fears of another writer's inevitable decline and death I was doing something that felt unseemly, taboo for very good reasons. When I am in my mid-fifties and full of plans and enjoying myself thoroughly, enjoying even the plaintive things I am beginning to write about age and about how one's best work antedates celebrity, will I want a writer twenty-five years younger than I to fret publicly about the fact that at some decades-distant point I am going to stop writing and die? No. In the preface to *Self-Consciousness*, Updike mentions his horror when somebody approached him to write his biography: "to take my life, my lode of ore and heap of memories, from me!" And someone, Updike or Anthony Powell I believe [or maybe Mailer?], mentions the "wariness"—I think that's the word—that older writers come to feel toward younger ones, a wariness that ought to be respected, I felt. Yet here I was, proposing to myself to steal Updike's very death-dread from him. It was a terrible idea. I hated that kind of cocky, unsubtle, overcandid irreverence in young writers. If I saw an essay in *The Atlantic* entitled "U and I" I would click my tongue with disgust and slap the magazine back deliberately in the wrong place on the newsstand rack, behind *Iron Horse* or *Needlecraft*. But would my irritable reaction be purely negative, or would it have a component of recognition, a wish that I had tried to do the same thing myself? And if it would have such a component of recognition, was that really a compelling reason for going ahead and writing it myself, rather than waiting for someone abler and less risk-averse than I to do it in his or her own way? Waiting was probably better.

For a full week after trying to reach the editor of *The Atlantic*, I occupied myself with other things. On October 31 I made some cheerful notes about Tracy Chapman's singing and about Bizet's *Carmen*. On the first of November I wrote at length about my ingrown toenail. But it just wasn't enough. Without some sort of anxiousness writing loses its charm. There is the straightforward suspense that is built into a certain kind of novel—a first-order plot-anxiety that I often dislike and find physically uncomfortable—and then there is the much more important second-order thrill that the writer himself shivers gleefully with as he writes: "Ooh boy, I'm really going to catch it this time! They're going to cremate me! I'm going to be pulverized!" (And then he does catch it, and he is stunned by how badly it hurts, and he never ignores that particular warning fear so completely again.) So, craving danger, looking up from my still-throbbing ingrown toenail, I called the editor of *The Atlantic* again on November 2. This time he was in, and, when I described the project to him in a low, worried voice, he was fairly agreeable. He and an agent worked out terms. The agent called me in the afternoon and told me that the editor had told her that he thought an essay such as I described about Updike could be good or it could be "very creepy."

At first "creepy" seemed a poor choice of word, but once I began writing in earnest, its aptness became increasingly apparent. What I was doing *was* creepy. Halloween was, after all, still in the air. Halloween is taken extremely seriously in the town where I live: there is a Halloween parade on Main Street at which policemen enthusiastically tamper with through traffic, and hundreds of children visit every lit house, and the local medium-security prison advertises to X-ray all bags of candy for harmful objects until 11:00 P.M. on the big night. My wife told me about the X-ray ad (which she had seen in the local free weekly) the morning after, and I was crazy with regret. If John *Updike* were thirty-two years old and living in this town, I thought, he would have known beforehand about that incredible X-ray offer and he would have driven up there with his kids after going trick-or-treating with them and he would have talked affably with the prison guard about some of the concealed weaponry the guard had found in gifts to prisoners and whether there had ever in fact been any adulterated candy of any kind detected locally or whether it was simply a mythical precautionary thing intended to demonstrate the prison's wish to contribute in whatever way it could to the happiness and welfare of the community in which it found itself, and Updike would have slyly looked around and caught a little flavorsome garniture of the X-ray room, perhaps a sign whose text would look funny in small caps, and he would maybe have jotted down a few comments his kids made as the image of the nuts in the miniature Snickers bars and the internal segmentation in the Smarties packets appeared on the gray screen, and then he would have driven home and in less than an hour produced a nice *Talk of the Town* piece that worked understatedly through the low-grade ghoulishness of driving to a medium-security prison to have your children's Halloween candy X-rayed for razor blades, in an epoch when apples were so completely *not* a Halloween treat anymore, and when all candy bars had tamper-evident wrappers. No, no, worse than that: he wouldn't have done it when he was thirty-two; he would have done it, better than I can do it now, when he was *twenty-five.* At thirty-two it would have been beneath him, too easy, too reportorial, too much of a typical Talk piece, whereas for me, I thought, it has the feeling of an outstanding topic, full of the exciting timeliness of nonfiction magazine writing. *I*, at thirty-two, had missed the story completely; the only piece (I dislike that journalismoid word "piece," and yet it slips in all the time) I could possibly do was one about wanting to have written a bright little prison-visit piece: that is, about the adulterating of innocent children's holidays by the writer's hyperreceptivity to newsworthy small-town touches—and who would want to read that? I wanted so much to have the assured touch, the adjectival resourcefulness, that Updike had in all his occasional writings; for though early on he eloquently disparaged the "undercooked quality of prose written to order," the truth was that some of his finest moments were to be found in the aforementioned introductions, awards-acceptance speeches, answers to magazine surveys, the last sentences of reviews (like the one that leaps, blurb-driven, to memory concerning Nabokov's *Glory*: "In its residue of bliss experienced, and in its charge of bliss conveyed, *Glory* measures up as, though the last to arrive, far from the least of this happy man's Russian novels"—terrifying mastery!), prefaces to his own writings, dedications (like the one that I think about all the time, in *Problems and Other Stories*, to his children, which includes the phrase "with the curve of sad time it subtends"—imagine him applying high school geometry to the mess of his own divorce in such a perfect figure!): those incidental forms that induce his verbal tact to close around some uncomfortable chip of reality even as it reaches to reawaken our dulled sense of why certain conventions (like book dedications) or stock phrases (like "last but not least") exist and what limber life can be found in them; those forms whose mastery seems to me to be more convincing proof of the spontaneity of true talent, its irrepressive oversupply, than any single master-piece is; and forms which for emulous younger writers can be more important as objects of study than the triple-deckers they besprinkle, because they are clues to the haberdashery of genius, its etiquette, its points of specific contact with the recognizable obligations of life, independent of some single lucky choice of subject that bigger forms such as the novel demand. But even as I saw the huge importance of incidental work to the presence, the coloring, the perceived surplusage, of the man of letters, I found that I was less and less able to imagine myself producing it with anything like the fertile freshness that Updike demonstrated almost weekly. In theory I resist the campy adult celebration of Halloween; and in theory I reject Harold Bloom's allegories of literary influence and parricide and one-upmanship (of which more later, I hope); but when I heard that the editor of *The Atlantic* had said that what I was doing sounded "creepy," and when I thought again of another of Updike's phrases from *Self-Consciousness* that somebody quoted in a review, "Celebrity is a mask that eats into the face," I realized that like it or not I was clearly risking with this essay the charge that I was simply engaged in a little trick-or-treating of my own on Updike's big white front porch.

3

"Well!" said my parents, independently. "If you're writing about Updike you'll have to go back and read everything he's written!" But in the midst of my various Halloween uncertainties and forebodings, the fact that I should *not* supplement or renew my impressions with fresh draughts of Updike was the one thing of which I was absolutely sure. I was not writing an obituary or a traditional critical study, I was trying to record how one increasingly famous writer and his books, read and unread, really functioned in the fifteen or so years of my life since I had first become aware of his existence as I sat at the kitchen table on a Sunday afternoon, watching with envious puzzlement my mother laugh harder than I had ever seen her laugh before (except at a Russell Baker column a few years earlier) as she read an Updike essay on golf in a special edition of *The New York Times Book Review*. Unlike her laughter at my slow-motion imitations of drivers undergoing head-on collisions, or at my father's mimed weight-lifting routines, or at my sister's sudden pretend facial tics while doing a barre, my mother's delight that Sunday had no charity or encouragement in it: it was miraculous, sourced in the nowhere of print, unaided by ham mannerisms; it caused her to spill her tea. She tried to read me some of it—"A divot the size of . . . a divot the size of an undershirt . . ."—but she couldn't, it was too funny. Nothing is more impressive than the sight of a complex person suddenly ripping out a laugh over some words in a serious book or periodical. I took note of *The New York Times Book Review* after that day, and I began increasingly to want to be a part of the prosperous-seeming world of books (prosperous in contrast, that is, to the grant-dependent and sparsely attended concerts for living composers, whose ranks I had up until then wanted to join), where there was money for screaming full-page ads and where success was quantified as it was on the Billboard charts, and where consequently there didn't seem to be quite the enormous gulf between popular and elite efforts as there was in music. Indeed, Updike himself regularly appeared *on* the best-seller list! Could anyone claim that Elliot Carter or Morton Subotnick or Walter Piston or John Cage or even Gian-Carlo Menotti was a complete tweeter-woofer-crossover success in the way that Updike was? It looked as if (this was mid-seventies) classical music was at one of the very lowest points of its postbaroque harmonic cycle, and I knew I didn't have anything like the talent someone would need to yank it out of its slump single-handedly.

Fiction, on the other hand, was a regular block party! People evidently had things to say with words, and other people appeared to be willing to read them. Fueled by this primitive observation, I began to write fiction in December of 1976, when I was nineteen and on leave from college. For Christmas my mother gave me *Picked-Up Pieces*, a collection that included the golf essay that had cracked her up a few years earlier: she said she liked the cover a lot, which was a wide-angle black-and-white shot of Updike in his front yard holding out a handful of fallen leaves. I was secretly disappointed by the gift, because I wanted to own paperback fiction, not hardback collections of book reviews, and I threw out the jacket because I wanted the hardback books I did have on my shelf to look more like the books in university libraries, which, unlike the embarrassingly crinkly tenants of public institutions, weren't shelved with their jackets on. But I did read some of it, starting with the interviews in the back and the essay near the beginning called "On Meeting Writers"—in it I read his account of having tea with Joyce Cary, who mentioned James Joyce and E. E. Cummings with approval. "I absurdly shook my head No," Updike says, and immediately I wondered whether I would ever write anything as good as that phrase, with its adverb so economically dropped in. And since that Christmas of 1976 I have been reading Updike very intermittently, but thinking about him constantly, comparing myself with him, using my inventory of remembered phrases and scenes in his writing as touchstones—some negatively, but most positively charged. Writing this reminds me of a touching fritter from the preface to Gilbert Murray's *Ancient Greek Literature*: ". . . for the past ten years at least, hardly a day has passed on which Greek poetry has not occupied a large part of my thoughts, hardly one deep or valuable emotion has come into my life which has not been either caused, or interpreted, or bettered by Greek poetry." Hardly a day has passed over the last thirteen years in which Updike has not occupied at least a thought or two; and while his constant summonings were at the outset brought on more by skeptical ambition than by simple enjoyment, the enjoyment and admiration were increasingly there as well.

And yet, shockingly, I've read fewer than five pages of:

Rabbit Is Rich
Buchanan Dying
S.
Tossing and Turning
Telephone Poles

Fewer than twenty pages of:

Roger's Version
A Month of Sundays
The Carpentered Hen
Bech Is Back
Midpoint

Assorted Prose
Couples

Less than half of:

The Witches of Eastwick
The Coup
Problems
Trust Me

While I have read more than half of:

Marry Me
Bech: A Book
Hugging the Shore
The Centaur
Self-Consciousness
Picked-Up Pieces

And I've read most or all of:

Pigeon Feathers
Of the Farm
The Poorhouse Fair
Rabbit, Run
Rabbit Redux
The Music School
Museums and Women
The Same Door

This man, you say, *is parading his ignorance! This man is taking up precious space writing about Updike when he admits to having read less than half the words Updike has written! It's not a disarming admission, it's an enraging admission!* But this very spottiness of coverage is, along with the wildly untenable generalizations that spring from it, one of the most important features of the thinking we do about living writers: as with nearby friends we seldom see because their very proximity removes the pressing need to drop by, so the living writer's continuing productivity dulls any urgent feelings we might have about filling in our unread gaps in his oeuvre. When he's dead we suddenly scramble to make our knowledge whole. Nor does the large proportion of early Updike on the "most or all" list above imply a straightforward value judgment: I am most interested in the books Updike wrote when he was my age or younger, because these are the ones whose problems I stand the best chance of understanding; the older I get, the more drawn I expect to be by his later books.

No, I couldn't possibly read Updike chronologically through right now: it would irreparably harm the topography of my understanding of him. A multiplicity of examples would compete to illustrate a single point, in place of the one example that had made the point seem worth making in the first place; the restiveness of obligation would warp my likings; I'd try to come up with recherché proofs

of Updike's greatness rather than the ones I really believe
in; I would in some cases possibly be disappointed by the
immediate context of a phrase I loved, when the context
was now hazy and irrelevant—indeed, the very readiness of
certain phrases to shrug off their contexts and take their
place as cherished independent inhabitants of my private
florilegia was part of what I liked so much about them, as
witness the infinite colorful magician's handkerchief of years
that is pulled from the inkwell in "A Sense of Shelter," and
especially that very first phrase I'd noted down on August
6: "vast dying sea." In an early story a character leans his
forehead against a bookcase, and considers "all the poetry
he had once read evaporating in him, a vast dying sea." It's
a stupendous moment in the story, in fiction, perfectly sit-
uated (at least so I remember it), but I think its stupen-
dousness derives in part from its own plucky ability to stay
afloat, like a lifesaving scrap of Queequeg's coffin, as the rest
of the story and almost all of literature capsizes and decays
in deep corrosive oceans of totaled recall. I remember almost
nothing of what I read. What once was *Portrait of a Lady*
is now for me only a plaid lap-blanket bobbing on the waves;
Anna Karenina survives as a picnic basket containing a single
jar of honey; *Pnin* is a submerged aquamarine bowl; *The
Rock Pool*'s cab meter still ticks away, showing a huge sum,
but the Mediterranean has overtaken the rest of the resort
town of Trou-sur-Mer; an antelope from some otherwise

blank Christopher Isherwood short story springs wonder-
fully up out of oblivion "like a grand piano"; the ample
landfall I think I have sighted in *Paradise Lost* turns out only
to be the "scaly rind" of the Leviathan in the first canto;
and even Alan Hollinghurst's stunning *The Swimming-Pool
Library*, which I am right now in the process of reading,
haven't yet finished, have no excuse for forgetting, already
hangs suspended in my inhospitable memory merely as a
group of sodden "sticking plasters" fluttering, as he describes
them, like an undersea plant near the grate of a water filter.
My quality of recollection may well be more atomistically
image-hoarding than some, yet the twice-ten-thousand-
cavern-glutting expanse and depth of the "vast dying sea"
of the once read, over which we all permanently and cheer-
fully row and pole and sail according to our talents, unless
our sense of a particular work is falsely stimulated by review
writing, the commemorative essay, teaching, an imminent
exam, or the hasty once-over that a dinner guest seems to
feel is necessary before he or she meets the writer after a
long interval, is the most important feature of all reading
lives. And if we want to know how we think about a writer
without the artifice of preparation, how we think about
Updike in particular only when we *discover ourselves* thinking
about him, when some feature of the world or of our own
thoughts spontaneously recalls a tone or tick or glimpse of
his work, or even merely brings up the image of his face in

a particular jacket photo (like the *Poorhouse Fair* shot of him sitting on a bench in which my mother thought he looked too pleased with himself) or the memory of some fifth-hand story one has heard or read about him—if we want *that* sort of elusive knowledge, even rereading a paragraph or a line while our meditation was in progress would be fatal to our oceanography. Indeed, my current aversion to seeing any printed word by Updike has reached such superstitious heights that, just as once several years ago I opened *Hugging the Shore* to the index and announced to myself, "If I don't find an entry for J. K. Huysmans in this index, I will be a better writer than Updike" (I did find one, unfortunately), so lately I've been saying to myself, "If I accidentally read a direct sentence of Updike's—not one that I have remembered on my own, but a real sentence set in type in a book or a magazine—while I'm writing this essay, the essay will turn out to be terrible and will never be published in *The Atlantic* or anywhere else." But sadly, while I was at a used book store one evening two weeks ago, I was drawn uncontrollably to the Updike shelf, and I saw there a Franklin Library edition of *Rabbit, Run*. I wrestled with temptation—I had never before looked over an example of Franklin's facture, and I had been fascinated by Updike's "special message" accompanying the Franklin Library edition of *Marry Me*, reprinted in *Hugging the Shore*, where he mentions a bookcase he's just finished building and painting, whose dents and defects will in time come to seem inevitable and comfortably comely, even as the flaws in *Marry Me* itself will undergo a parallel transformation, and I wanted to know if this edition of *Rabbit, Run* had some front matter I had not read. Finally my resistance collapsed and I pulled the weighty collector's volume off the shelf. The padded, bright red binding was somewhat more reminiscent of a comfortable corner booth at an all-night, all-vinyl coffee shop than one might have thought fitting for so aggressively "classic" an enterprise; but even so a bible-ready black fabric bookmark did curl with high seriousness out of the gilt-edged, acid-free solidity of the massed pages like a dried umbilicus: I said, "Wow!"—moved to mingled feelings of tenderness and stern disapproval by the prematurely ornate, bootstrappingly heirloomish, "undercooked" look it had, and I was unable to keep from opening it up. Within I saw a *Reader's Digest*ive illustration of boys playing basketball, and then, as I turned the title page, my iris unwittingly allowed entry to several words from the opening sentence, thereby shattering all my fond hopes for the success of this essay—unless, *unless*, I deviously told myself, there was a way to include a confession of this very lapse in that part of my case study which mentioned how studiously and superstitiously I had otherwise avoided any rereading. That might work to fend off the bad omen! In his promptly funereal study of Zola (appearing in *The Atlantic* in August of 1903), Henry James at one point forces himself to admit that he hasn't been able to reread every one of Zola's novels while preparing himself for the job at hand: "There are efforts here at stout perusal that, frankly, I have been unable to carry through," he confesses. I liked the idea that I, by contrast with Henry James, would have "frankly" to admit that I *had* happened to reread, contrary to all my severe resolutions, a single opening clause from one of Updike's novels; the courageousness of that admission would somehow leave the seal over my own naturally pickled long-term "dying sea" memories of Updike acceptably intact.

(But this isn't *Religio Medici*; Browne's casualness with direct quotation is not possible now: when I finished the entire essay I assembled all my Updike books, and I took out from the library the ones I lacked, and I tried to locate each phrase I had used. In most cases I regretfully corrected my misquotations—regretfully because my errors of memory were themselves of mild scientific interest to me. During my searches I had to stave off the intense desire to bolster the argument with other quotations I encountered along the way. A surprising number of phrases weren't where I remembered them as being—for example, I was sure that "vast dying sea," which I encountered in 1982, was in "Who Made Yellow Roses Yellow," but I finally found it in "Incest." And I *knew* that his sentence about reading "what they told me" in college was in *Esquire*'s 1989 summer reading issue—it isn't. Where my argument depends in some way on my misquotation, I have left the error intact and simply corrected myself between brackets: []. If the phrase was not to be found anywhere in a week of flipping and skimming, I resorted to "Updike says something like" and kindred fudgings to indicate that what I'm remembering is only a paraphrase, and may not even exist.)

I was definitely planning to put my Updike thoughts in some order—I was going to do them *that* injustice, at least—but as I tallied and itemized and found links between the phrases I remembered or misremembered from his books, I realized how fortunate I was in one important respect: though our man had already taken his place on a page of Bartlett's, no quirk of fame had yet singled out even one tag phrase that would have overinsistently interposed itself between my private recollections of his work and the sort of Familiar Quotation memory-at-large that culture eventually requires as the price of its permanent attention, or simply so as not to be overwhelmed by the infinitude of every literary personality. If I were to pop-quiz myself, right now, "Hey, what about Henry's brother, old William James—what do I think of him?"—the irritating bluebottle phrase "blooming buzzing confusion" would be first to answer my solicitation, and it would be impossible to wave away, once summoned, in that thought-session. Years of reflection, faculty meetings, mood shifts, changes of profession, trips to Europe, religious doubts, letters from his brother, sensory information of the most varied sort—all of it has been compacted into words that now (through simple overquotation, to which I guiltily contribute here) have no more intrinsic bloom or buzz or confusion than a spherical rabbit dropping suspended in a pyramidal lucite paperweight. And yet when William James comes to mind unbidden, what I think of most often is a time in New York City during the penny shortage of 1981 when the McDonald's on Seventieth and Second was offering, so a huge sign said in the window, a free Big Mac to every customer who exchanged five dollars' worth of pennies for a five-dollar bill. I pulled the blankets off my bed and on the smoothness of the bottom sheet counted out five one-hundred-penny piles from the copper reserves I had accumulated in barely a year and had stored in a number of glass custard cups and other amphorae in my room. The pennies so grouped I scooped into five plastic bags, and with my pounds of spare change and an anthology of William James's writing that I had taken out of the library that very day in hand, I walked to the McDonald's and waited my turn. But as I slowly drew closer to the cash registers, my elation and amusement at taking McDonald's up on their offer (and thereby getting a rate of return on my residual earnings, roughly $1.50 on $5.00 over a year's time, that would have made any mutual fund proud) began to sift away: I was right in the middle of the dinner rush, and there were many rich-looking cashmere-coated women behind me in line whose tempers would snap if my pennies added a further delay. As I feared, when my turn came, the manager was called over, and despite my repeated claims that he didn't have to count the pennies, that there really were five hundred of them there, he poured out each plastic bag in turn and slid its contents two by two off the counter and into his palm, while beads of sweat appeared on his brow, and the cooking machines beeped their blood-pressure-heightening appeals behind him, and cash drawers sprang open and were pelvised closed and rushed order takers skated around on several mashed french fries under-foot—for this guy was only the manager on duty; he had only inherited the free-Mac offer, he hadn't conceived of it, he had at most taped up the sign, and he evidently didn't comprehend its motive, which was the overridingly urgent need for pennies, in bulk, their precise numbers to be de-termined at the close of business in the leisure of the back office, and not while dozens of well-off, exhausted East Sid-ers curled their lips at my somehow pathetic miserliness, and especially at the sight of my humiliatingly domestic plastic sandwich bags, which looked so out of place, so homemade, slumped anonymously on a counter where every carton and wrapper and cup had a ratifying logo printed on it, as if my bags enclosed stale trouvailles I'd discovered poking through the trash after a church bake sale, or ancient concave baloney sandwiches that my mother had made for me to take to grade school and that I had hoarded all these years in jabbering archivalism—as if, in other words, I was, in my indigent desperation, trying to pawn some unlovely private collection, of value only to me, in exchange for food. When the pennies were finally all counted and I got the free Big Mac and a paid-for drink to go with it, I was fuchsia not only with primary embarrassment but with a secondary more agonizing humiliation at not having been able to pull off this unchallenging public moment without blushing: I reeled to the violently yellow "dining room," and to escape any stares at my facial coloring I bent very low over the William James book, which I opened randomly at a selection from *The Principles of Psychology*.

But the moment I began eating, my mortification reversed its engines and transformed itself into a fierce desire to gloat: I was chewing my way through something substantial, tiered, sweet, meaty, that had cost everyone else in the room money but which I had gotten for free. I had a five-dollar bill in my wallet that I hadn't had before: McDonald's was *paying me* to eat here! I wanted to laugh a wicked mean pitiless insane laugh, the kind that some bums, who for some reason always found the sight of me funny, would often helplessly produce, shaking their heads, pointing a finger, as my too-tall, wire-rimmed, pinheaded form caught their dissolutely untetrahydrozolinable eye: among bums I felt like an established and salaried Upper East Sider, but among Upper East Siders, I felt I had hugely swollen ankles and tattered back issues of magazines projecting from several pockets and dirty bandages hanging by one wing on my face. And contributing at least half of this joyful inburst was William James himself, who, it turned out, was *really good*: unpretentious, jolly, at his ease—as smart as, but completely different from, his brother. I came to a page with an illustration—a number of shaky curved lines all traveling by different routes from a point A to a point Z—meant to illustrate the various paths that the recently christened, pre-Joycean "stream of thought" might take in moving from one established idea to another. It was a glorious sight. The confident, lighthearted didacticism of this small drawing made me shake my head with instant affection for William James; I thought of him frowning over it, attempting to capture by the tremble in his execution the irregular uniqueness of each thought path, prouder of this artwork perhaps than the prose that led up to it, because his first wish had been to become a painter; and I thought of those several contemporary illustrators whose style was based on the same trembly, Dow-Jonesy contour line: William Steig, for instance, and Seymour Chwast, and whoever did that Alka-Seltzer cartoon commercial in the sixties in which (as I remembered it) a yiddishly unhappy human stomach, gesticulating from an analyst's couch or chair, its esophagus waggling like an unruly forelock, told its troubles to a nodding murmuring doctor; and I thought also of the frail, capelli d'angelesque decorative markings a professor of philosophy at Haverford, Richard Bernstein, used to leave behind on the chalkboard as he "gave some texture to" an argument in Popper, Lakatos, or Paul Feyerabend—filaments of faint connectivity that visually supplemented the lengthy meditative "ee-ee-ee-ee" noise that he used to extend his favorite transitional phrase, "in a certain sort of way." *In a certain sort of way-ee-ee-ee.* Now, when William James enters my thoughts unexpectedly, the accompanying image most often takes this form, as the sight of the drawing on that right-hand page on that evening at McDonald's. And yet the major coincidence of the occasion—the explicit exchange of pennies for thoughts, the sudden, specially sauced incarnation on Seventieth Street of that formerly empty saying—did not make itself felt to me until this year, as I worked on my second novel, in which small change figured, against my will, as a minor theme, and I finally recognized, with disappointment conjoined with gratitude, that this previous William Jamesian memory explained to some degree *why* pennies and their brethren seemed so strangely evocative to me; disappointment, of course, because one always wants one's fascinations to come originally from life and not from the library. And when, this year as well, I made some small-time publicity appearances in connection with my first novel and was typically, Americanly inarticulate—indeed, worse than typical: tongue-tied, "um"-saying, jargon-ridden, flat-voweled—when I saw the eyes of the radio interviewess widen in alarm as the stretch of dead air lengthened, and when I compared myself miserably with an amazing performance by Updike on Dick Cavett that I recalled from the late seventies, where he spoke in swerving, rich, complex paragraphs of unhesitating intelligence that he finally allowed to glide to rest at the curb with a little downward swallowing smile of closure, as if he almost felt that he ought to apologize for his inability even to fake the need to grope for his expression, and for inspiring the somewhat frantic efforts Cavett made to keep archly abreast of this unoratorical, uncrafty, *generous* precision; and when I compared my awkward public self-promotion too with a documentary about Updike that I saw in 1983, I believe, on public TV, in which, in one scene, as the camera follows his climb up a ladder at his mother's house to put up or take down some storm windows, in the midst of this tricky physical act, he tosses down to us some startlingly lucid little felicity, something about "These small yearly duties which blah blah blah," and I was stunned to recognize that in Updike we were dealing with a man so naturally verbal that he could write his fucking memoirs *on a ladder!*—when, as I say, I compared myself very unfavorably to Updike's public manner after my own radio disasters (I heard myself over the car radio and had to pull over on a side street and get out and shut the door on my upstate voice, which I was tape-recording), I repeatedly comforted myself with a thing against spoken eloquence from Addison that I had read in Boswell: "I have but ninepence in my pocket," it roughly goes, "but I can draw on a thousand pounds"; and the fiscal simile here too attached itself to my idea of William James, whom I thought of, wrongly no doubt, as struggling for expression, or at least for a form proper to his style of reasoning, while his gay brother unfumblingly dictated sentence after incredible sentence to his typist.

"Blooming buzzing confusion." "Hard, gemlike flame." "Hobgoblin of little minds." "The terrible *fluidity* of self-revelation." "I refute it thus." They're all dead and fully folded away, accessible by one or two of these handy pull tabs, in the thick faded Harper Torchbook of intellectual history. But not only is Updike himself physically alive, his writing feels alive as well: it's still in constant democratic motion, unteachable, not in equilibrium, free to organize itself around any particular scene or image or pronouncement, no standardized ID phrase yet dangling from a protruding morgued toe. I find myself speculating, in fact, what phrase will become the jingle we will have to fight past at some point in the future to reawaken our real pleasures in Updike. From *Self-Consciousness* reviewers quoted "Celebrity is a mask that eats into the face," and there is a certain memorable shock in that, but it's too downbeat to represent his tone adequately. When I asked my mother what she remembered from Updike, the first thing she mentioned was the sentence about divorce from the foreword to *Too Far to Go*: "That a marriage ends is less than ideal; but all things end under heaven, and if temporality is held to be invalidating, then nothing real succeeds." She's absolutely right, it should be in the next edition of Bartlett's. And Nabokov long ago quoted admiringly a beautiful, beautiful phrase from one story: "Their conversation was like a basket woven underwater around a useless stone." [No no no— the sentence really goes: "The important thing, rather than the subject, was the conversation itself, the quick agreements, the slow nods, the weave of different memories; it was like one of those Panama baskets shaped underwater around a worthless stone."] Perhaps that too will become one of Updike's tags, since its image by example so nicely defuses the tiresome criticism that he doesn't have any-thing—that is, any useless stone [no, *worthless* stone—there's a difference] of exotic experience—to write about. But meanwhile, lucky for me, there is no aphoristic consensus to deflect and distort the trembly idiosyncratic paths each of us may trace in the wake of the route that the idea of Updike takes through our consciousnesses.

4

One such tracing might begin, for instance, at the 125th anniversary party for *The Atlantic*, held in the fall of 1982. I rented a black tie outfit and went with my now-wife. We stood on the black-and-white tiled basement floor of the Marriott Long Wharf, relieved to see that the crowd was much too big for us to be expected to talk to anyone. I said things like "Are those what are known as 'spaghetti straps'?" indicating with my chin a woman whose back was to us, and my now-wife said things like "Almost: those over there are"—and we nodded and laughed exaggeratedly, as if we hadn't taken a cab there together but had met for the first time in years at this grand function. And yet after forty-five minutes, the pressure, slight at first but growing, to have at least one extra-dyadic conversation that I could use to imply hours of raucous socializing in later accounts, began to make me glance around with more purpose. I began to feel slightly desperate. We were forced to eat sliced and stuffed things at traypoint: each time the tray came around I felt that the bearer was adding another yes checkmark to his suspicion that we had arrived and talked to nobody but ourselves. Finally an assistant editor introduced us to Judith Martin, Miss Manners, who had been deep in real, unfeigned conversation with somebody else. She, understandably revolted by our foolish beaming pleading miserable faces, and put off by the borderline rudeness of the person who had performed the introduction, since he had failed to take into account how very deep her preexisting conversation had been, apparently felt that it was her duty as a syndicated upholder of social norms not to talk to us or nod kindly at us or even to look at us until we could demonstrate that we were comfortable and capable in this sort of expensive literary ceremony—perhaps at *The Atlantic*'s 130th anniversary party (which I wasn't invited to anyway). I looked at her intelligent, appealing profile, and in the midst of my sincere discomfiture ("shitting and pissing in terror," as William Burroughs might say) I was grateful to her, for my now-wife and I now had a story to tell: Miss Manners had cut us dead. We backed away. I spotted Tim O'Brien. "There's Tim O'Brien!" I hissed. "Finally somebody I know!" We hustled over. He'd forgotten me. He (*Going after Cacciato*, National Book Award, 1979) had been one of the faculty in a two-week writer's conference at Berkeley in 1981; I'd been a student in Donald Barthelme's class at the same conference. "So why are you here?" Tim O'Brien asked, rather brutally.

I told him we lived in Boston and that I'd had some things in *The Atlantic*. He nodded. We all looked around, nodded approvingly at the hors d'oeuvres, looked around again. A feeling of major literary power was in the room, but it was difficult to locate it in any one person. "Is Updike here?" I asked.

Tim O'Brien said something like "I don't know. I haven't seen him."

"I haven't either."

My now-wife shook her head: she hadn't seen Updike either.

"Bellow's supposedly here," said Tim O'Brien.

"Yes, so I heard," I said. "I was wondering about Updike, though. They would have invited him, don't you think? I mean he had a story, 'Pygmalion,' in the magazine fairly recently."

Tim O'Brien thought Updike probably would have been invited. And then he dropped his bomb. "I go golfing with Updike."

"*Really?*"

"Yeah, we go golfing. It's kind of nice. But he has one rule: no talk about books."

We nodded—wise, very wise. Updike didn't make an appearance at the party, but this short exchange with Tim O'Brien, especially coming just after our devastating but dine-out-on-able failure with Miss Manners (who func-

tioned allegorically for me as the bouncer at the porte co-
chere of the cultural establishment), was more than enough
literary ferment for one evening. I was of course very hurt
that out of all the youngish writers living in the Boston area,
Updike had chosen Tim O'Brien and not me as his golfing
partner. It didn't matter that I hadn't written a book that
had won a National Book Award, hadn't written a book of
any kind, and didn't know how to golf: still, I felt strongly
that Updike should have asked me and not Tim O'Brien.
That "astounded" ball and the "divot the size of an undershirt" in Updike's golf essay that had made my mother laugh
so hard were what had first switched my attention from
music to writing. I was clubable! And I knew that he had
read me, because the year before, an editor at *The New Yorker*
wrote me saying that Updike had seen my story there and
had asked who I was. And now, by 1982, with a full four
short stories published, I thought my writing could plausibly
claim a peak metaphorical infusion rate closer to Updike's
own than Tim O'Brien's (though I had scarcely read O'Brien
then). It was true that I hadn't done anything in that line
anywhere near as good as Updike's description of the large
block of ice in *Rabbit, Run*, with its eraser markings leading
the eye deep into the white exploding star at the center, or
the "cool margins of the bed" in *The Centaur*, but that, and
not the expert storyteller's pacing of *Going after Cacciato*,
was clearly the direction I was going to improve in if I

improved at all. The metaphors I came up with might well turn out to be "pushed," in the very worrisome adjective Updike used in a review of *Blue Highways*, but there were going to be lots of them, at least at the beginning. (The metaphorical sense, along with the flea-grooming visual acuity that mainly animates it, fades in importance over most writing careers, replaced, with luck, by a finer social attunedness—although in a story from 1987 [or rather 1986—"The Afterlife"] Updike has a tossed-off description of an excitable horse's "gelatinous" eyeball that still outsees everyone else writing.) But wasn't the very gulf of method that separated O'Brien and Updike the point, I asked myself? If Updike was going to choose a golf-buddy from the ranks of existing writers, relative recognition or merit or promise aside, wasn't he more likely to choose someone whose bag of tricks was different enough from his own to keep that natural rivalrousness, that "wariness," as much at bay as possible?

It may seem incredible, given how little I had published and how bad it was, that I could have even idly theorized as to why Updike wasn't making an effort to seek me out, but I did. I was puzzled as well by his need to golf with a writer. One of the things I had admired about him was his deliberate self-removal from New York, and his unwillingness to participate in writer's conferences or accept academic appointments or get himself involved in that whole tragic, talent-draining process whereby writers cluster together to attract aspirants who pay big money in exchange for some chumminess and advice (meanly I call it tragic, when I had been very willing to write out a check for hundreds of dollars in order to gain the audience of Donald Barthelme, and I had had a wonderful time!): yet here Updike was seeking out another writer to play golf with. It was that frigging National Book Award, I thought: that was the ticket into his esteem. But this was ridiculous. There were many explanations, aside from Tim O'Brien's simple likability. Updike was perhaps even then working on the essay about his pro-Vietnam-war activities, and he might well have been interested in getting to know somebody articulate who knew as much about Vietnam firsthand as O'Brien did. He could have already *done* the nonliterary golf-buddy thing and found that even with a strict prohibition against bookchat, even if they only talked about cars or the resale market for dredged golf balls or urban renewal programs, a writer was a more engaging companion to clump from hole to hole with than some division manager from Digital. Still, it was this anti-bookchat rule that especially focused my resentment. "Yup, we're going to pretend we're two regular guys," is how I first interpreted it. Imagine having a *rule* of conversation. Jeezamarooni! If I were out there with Updike on the fairway right now, and he had laid down that rule, I would, between bogeys, be coming out with nervous snickering references to Richard Yates and Patrick Süskind and Julian Barnes, just to test his tolerance of me as a golf partner—just to see if he would *make an exception for me*.

And yet of course I saw why the prohibition was necessary. When you spend a fair amount of time writing about other people's books, or making sure to steer clear in your own books of images or scenes that you remember from other people's books, you naturally don't want in your off hours to cover the same ground with all the diminishing slackness and imprecision of conversation. You're trying to be as different as possible from everyone else, as Frost more or less said, and you don't want any influences to travel back and forth in advance of the demonstrable influences you supply and receive in the public world of print. (Plus there must be a kind of small thrill in feeling the power in yourself to be able to set a rule of conversation: feeling the unsettling authority of saying, "But Tim, I do think we should follow one rule . . .") If *I* were golfing with Updike this week, would I tell him, "Hey, I'm reading Alan Hollinghurst's *The Swimming-Pool Library*, and you know, once you get used to the initially kind of disgusting level of homosexual sex, which quickly becomes really interesting as a kind of ethnography, you realize that this is really one of the best first novels to come along in years and years! The guy does everything—dialogue, scenic pageantry, wit, pathos, everything!" I would want to tell him this, but I wouldn't, I don't think, because what if by some chance Updike hadn't read Hollinghurst yet, and what if my say-so, the last of many, was just enough to make his eye pause on this book in the Vintage catalog and order it, and what if he read it and its presence in his mind caused him to shift his writing ever so slightly in a particular direction either toward or away? Or, alternatively, what if Updike found me irritating enough as a person that my ravings about Hollinghurst dimmed his own previous excitement about the book? Would I want to have tampered casually with his literary development, his *fate*, in that way? And what if he mentioned that he'd been rereading Shaftsbury and liking him, or rereading Wallace Stevens and liking him less? For months afterward, this bit of inside information would be the first thing I would think of in connection with these artists: I would read them with a slightly different eye, and I might as a result write differently. So no talk about books. But it was much worse than that. Could John Updike and I talk about cars or self-doubts or the weather? About the psoriasis we have in common?

Say he and I were golfing, and I was getting the hang of it a little better, and the birds were supplying their own spatial illusions to the sound track, and I suddenly came out with "Wow, John—*golf*. Now I see why you like it so much. It's an externalized battle with your skin. Your job as a golfer and as a psoriatic is to keep from drifting into the rough, right? You want to arrive as efficiently as possible at the finest, smoothest section of grass!" Say I said this fairly dumb thing to him one balmy afternoon. (Crossing my fingers, in doing so, in the hope that it wasn't something he himself had written that I had forgotten.) And what if a few years later he has occasion to write another golf story—some masterfully pastoral Byezhin Meadowy kind of thing—and the golf-course/psoriasis parallel occurs to him then, and he drops it in in a perfect spot, without the exclamation point, improved almost beyond recognition. Will I be happy to read this? Maybe eventually, but it will take some adjustment. As I say, I'm a psoriatic myself, and though Updike has said lots of what can be said about the disability, there is more, and there might come a time when I would want to have a scaly-rinded character imagine himself or herself as smooth as a golf course. So no—I couldn't talk about psoriasis with Updike: I'd be too scared of hearing something from him that I would itch to use before he'd used it, or of tempting him with a flake or two from my experience that I would want to keep for myself—or of hearing him say something similar to something I'd already noted down and was planning to use, and having my note killed by his passing mention. And I would sense his detection of all this ridiculous guardedness on my part: I would see him smiling to himself after I had begun to say something animated and then had halted abruptly and switched to a conventional formula because I had realized midway through that what

I had been intending to say was possibly interesting enough for me to want to use somewhere, or because I wanted to hustle him into thinking I was denser and more conventional than I was, so that he would relax and talk more freely, and so that I could surprise him later, making him think to himself when he read some *piece* of mine, "Hm, I guess that Nick Baker is not to be underestimated." Our very guard-edness and mutual suspicion, or at least my suspicion (or hope, rather) that the suspicion was mutual, would be an undertone of the outing that both of us might have our eye secretly on, to see whether there was anything in it that had an unsaid quality that could be transported effectively into print. Perhaps I would come right out and allude to my awareness of his potential wariness of me, just to see what happened, and he would reply that if there is wariness it is a middle phase and passes, as does the more specific hate you can feel toward young bright unsaddened people run-ning up and down the aluminum ladders of their own insides (in Forster's phrase) with no storm windows yet to change, no duties or sins to bend their chirping ambition in inter-esting ways, and that in fact you begin to take a sort of nostalgic joy in seeing that unrefined unwise reputationless rawness start to sort itself out, and you begin to find some amusement in watching a young writer prepare himself to do the small bold thing in the elder writer's presence, such as I had just done in alluding to his wariness, and that if I wrote with pretend farseeingness about my egotistical thought that he had a wistful wish to be me, he would counter by writing about his self-disgust at the pretense of generousness he'd shown in so breezily pretending that he didn't care whether I appropriated the complexities of that afternoon game of golf or not, and about the feeling you can have of *delegating* a piece of experience to someone, happy in the knowledge that though the idea of a biography's being produced about you is horrifying, the idea that someone is catching you in action from a perspective you'd never yourself have is pleasing. Quickly there would be a screech of feedback and the whole discussion would have to be cut short and I would be carted or caddied quickly off. Literary friendship is impossible, it seems; at least, it is impossible for me. Indeed, all male friendships outside of work sometimes seem to be impossible: you look at each other at the restaurant at some point in the conversation and you know that each of you is thinking, man, this is futile, why are we here, we're wasting our time, we have nothing to say, we're not involved in some project together that we can bitch about, we can't flirt, we feel like dummies discussing movies or books, we aren't in some moral bind with a woman that we need to confess, we've each said the other is a genius several times already, and the whole thing is depressing and the tone is false and we might as well go home to our wives and children and rent buddy movies like

Midnight Run or *Planes, Trains, and Automobiles* or *The Pope of Greenwich Village* when we need a shot of the old camaraderie. (Updike catches some of the false jocularity of reunions in a story about two ex-Harvard Lampoon types in New York, one of whom is angling for a job, in "Who Made Yellow Roses Yellow.") And yet I want to be Updike's friend now! Forget the guardedness! Helen Vendler once asked him in an interview about decorum and propriety and taste in poetry, and in particular about the sexual poems in a certain collection that seem a trifle indecorous. Updike said in reply that poetry is experienced in private, and that *life is too short* to worry about propriety. [His actual words, soaring miles above my ratty paraphrase, are: "I think taste is a social concept and not an artistic one. I'm willing to show good taste, if I can, in somebody else's living room, but our reading life is too short for a writer to be in any way polite. Since his words enter into another's brain in silence and intimacy, he should be as honest and explicit as we are with ourselves."] Well, life is too short to worry about a lot of things—reserve, tact, the advisability of saying in an essay that you are so miserly with your perceptions that you hesitate to imagine yourself golfing with another writer for fear that he would use something you said and that even so you still want very much to be friends with him. I *am* friends with Updike—that's what I really feel— I have, as I never had when I was a child, this imaginary friend I have constructed out of sodden crisscrossing strips of rivalry and gratefulness over an armature of remembered misquotation. Which leads me to a point that seems worth making. Friends, both the imaginary ones you build for yourself out of phrases taken from a living writer, or real ones from college, and relatives, despite all the waste of ceremony and fakery and the fact that out of an hour of conversation you may have only five minutes in which the old entente reappears, are the only real means for foreign ideas to enter your brain. If Hippocrates or Seneca, whom I know nothing about, says that art is long and life is short, it means little to me: it is merely an opinion some strangers have had and others have emptily quoted. But if Updike says that life is short, I feel the strength of it with something close to shock. The force of truth that a statement imparts, then, its prominence among the hordes of recorded observations that I may optionally apply to my own life, depends, in addition to the sense that it is argumentatively defensible, on the sense that someone like me, and someone I like, whose voice is audible and who is at least notionally in the same room with me, does or can possibly hold it to be compellingly true. Until a friend or relative has applied a particular proverb to your own life, or until you've watched him apply the proverb to his own life, it has no power to sway you.

In writing this down, however, with the usual disappointment at the pallor a once pressing idea finally assumes on my page, I notice that my account is incomplete: there was in reality a preliminary stage to my appreciation of Updike's truth that life is short. In 1985, an ex-professor put my name on the mailing list of writers to receive Guggenheim applications. I took the packet of cream-colored paper that came in the mail very seriously, because the Guggenheim was the only philanthropic grant that Updike had made use of: he wrote *The Centaur* with its help. (And I can't help suspecting that the odd artsy mythological chapters in that book, which is elsewhere so packed with visual delights, are there not only to introduce what he called "novelistic space," that feeling, as I understand the term, of having two or more processes going on concurrently among which the reader is shuttled, so that he forgets a little of each process in his exposure to the others, and feels the delight of re-acquaintance, and doesn't grow rebellious as quickly, but are there also to show the Guggenheimish world that this book is not merely a book about a kid worrying about the health of his father during a cold snap, which we couldn't *possibly* take seriously as the outcome of a financial award, but is a book fully aware of the myth criticism that so appealed to fifties literary folk. [I could not be more wrong in this theory: *Rabbit, Run*, it turns out, not *The Centaur* at all, was the book he wrote with a Guggenheim.]) But I was sure I wouldn't win the award and I was feeling very

doubtful about my writing in general and disliked the idea
of asking several people to write recommendations—that
awful moment I imagined in the phone call where the exchange of news falters and you say, "Another reason I'm
calling is . . ." and suddenly your real motives are laid bare:
you're *looking for a recommendation*, that's all, you wheedling
wretch, you don't really miss the professor or want to tell
him how much you still think about his class, you just want
further help in your dishonorable little battle up the grass-
blade toward some sort of eminence. Besides, the application
would only be complete and worth sending, to my mind,
if Updike was one of the ones who'd written a recommendation, and there was no way I could write Updike and ask
him to write me a recommendation based on the things I'd
had published. So I called my father-in-law (who'd won two
Guggenheims in history) to ask him what he thought about
going through with the application. I told him that I hated
to ask people for recommendations and that I doubted Updike would write me one and moreover (my voice here took
on a fluting, over-earnest tone) I was still in a very preparatory stage and I didn't feel I knew what I was doing well
enough yet to deserve a Guggenheim. He said that it was
virtuous of me to think that way (generously not pointing
out that I was much more pleased and unperplexed by the
appearance of this application in the mail than I pretended,
though including an almost imperceptible edge of chastise-

ment in his voice, there if I wanted to hear it, at what he easily saw was my transparently false modesty), but he said that if I thought that way for too long I'd "end up in heaven." I laughed, but I felt a moment of panic or rebuke—my father-in-law had always said that things had come early and easily for me, and now he was implying that I was getting older and putting things off and pretending to bemoan my imperfect apprenticeship. His voice, saying essentially, "But if you wait too long to apply for a Guggenheim your life will be over and you'll have done nothing," had the force it had because it was *his* voice, and because I fancied I could detect in it the always compelling tincture of veiled self-reproach: he regretted not writing more himself (so I crudely interpreted), regretted the wasteful rhythm of the academic year, which demands that half the summer be spent re-familiarizing oneself with the excitement one was just beginning to feel about one's chosen project by the end of the summer before, regretted how extremely much pleasure teaching itself gave him, even though he knew that its static sparks of eloquence robbed him of some of the stored voltage necessary to finish his next work of history; and his voice, in this sampled and stored and overinterpreted version, was what I mixed into the voice I heard a few years later when I read Updike saying, with that tone of almost impatient fatigue that often marks the high point of an interview with a writer, that life was too short to worry about propriety: in a momentary synthetic unison, these two men, one on the phone and the other on the page of *Hugging the Shore*, put a constructive fear of death in me. (I didn't apply for a Guggenheim, though.) Before you can accept it as true, you need to have the sensation, the illusion, that something is said directly *to you*, or that the idea has occurred to someone who resembles you enough to serve as your emotional plenipotentiary. And what a writer of an essay like this is trying to do, it now seems to me, is to cheat in a sense on this process: I'm trying to convince the reader that I'm such a stone-washed article that even lacking a recognized corpus or a biography or a remembered history of dorm-cafeteria conversation, or any known self outside of the one chunk of me here offered, I am somebody you know: we've been through the wars together, eaten at McDonald's, submitted to base motives, sweated through social gatherings, and so when I propose to tell you that John Updike is a genius, for example, my contention will have some trustworthy impulse of convincingness behind it.

5

In so explicitly combining Updike and my father-in-law in what I have just said, I am aware that I am probably begging for Harold Bloom's templates of literary patrimony to clamp confidently down on my life. But I haven't read any Harold Bloom, and all the way through writing this essay so far I have been experiencing bursts of anxiety about my ignorance of *The Anxiety of Influence*. Am I simply resaying things he's already said? "Adding texture"? I know about "misprision" only from book reviews—book reviews, not books, being the principal engines of change in the history of thought, and contributing in that necessary role a certain class of distortions to the forward flow by allowing those works which contain plots and arguments that are easily summarized in their reviews to assume a level of cultural bulk and threat that the books themselves may or may not deserve. It's not quite true to claim that I haven't read any Bloom: in 1982 I did read one thing, a very personal and (I now think) attractively exasperating introduction to the *Selected*

Writings of Walter Pater in which he claims that Pater's "only begetter" was Ruskin, whose anxiety-causing effect "can be read, frequently through negation, throughout Pater's work." I finally lost my temper ("You dipshit," I believe I said, slitting my eyes at the page) when I came to this snidely psychoanalytical sentence: "The overt influence [of Ruskin] Pater buried deep." But my dislike of "Pater buried deep" marked it in my memory for long-term storage, saving it from otherwise certain inundation—and now, in reaction to Bloom, I wish to unbury and acknowledge my debt in this essay to Bloom himself, who is in the air; but just as I can't read Updike now for fear that I would forfeit my one opportunity to represent as accurately as I can what I think of him when he comes to mind, and not when I summon him to mind, so I can't now study *The Anxiety of Influence* for fear that the book would take me over, remove the urgency I feel about what I'm recording here, transform the particulars of my relationship with Updike into a rather uninteresting instance of a powerful and already proven general law—necessarily less interesting than the relationship between Ruskin and Pater or Ruskin and Proust or Henry James and Proust or Proust and Beckett or Proust and Nabokov or Nabokov and Updike because unlike the rest of the illustrious terms in these comparisons, I am nobody—fame (not to speak of talent) hasn't conferred any external interest on my writhings. "Illustrious examples," Edward

Young wrote in 1760, in a passage that Bloom or his disciples have no doubt fixed on as an interesting prolepsis of the master's views, "*engross, prejudice*, and *intimidate*. They *engross* our attention, and so prevent a due inspection of ourselves; they *prejudice* our judgment in favour of their abilities, and so lessen the sense of our own; and they *intimidate* us with the splendour of their renown, and thus under diffidence bury our strength." Well, I will not be diffident—I will even go so far as to say that in this matter of treating how a person adapts to the tradition that precedes him I have been just as influenced by David Dreman's *Contrarian Investment Strategy* (a book I actually *have* read) as I have by the ideas of Harold Bloom that are in general invisible circulation. But why fight everyone's suspicion? I am writing *contre* Harold Bloom, like it or not, ignorant of his work or not, and in being so forthright about this I have to admit to feeling slightly superior to Updike, who surprised an early interviewer by naming Jack Kerouac as an inspiration. [Actually he merely said that of his contemporaries Kerouac "attempted to grab it all; somehow, to grab it all. I like him."] Kerouac? said the interviewer, in effect—just as Updike wanted him to. How *interesting*. And it may be that Kerouac's typing of *On the Road* on a roll of shelf paper or a piano roll or whatever the myth is was a spur to Updike, who had a suspicion that his descriptive polish wouldn't desert him even at full throttle and wanted to test its outer limits, after four years of the standard college rap about the sacredness of the act of revision. But I think we have to say that Kerouac *isn't* really the big influence, nor is Salinger, whom Updike shook after a few stories ("Janny!" calls a very Salingeresque girl in the first story he published)—the real influences (elsewhere freely admitted) are, regardless of respective ages, Nabokov, Proust, and later, perhaps, after he underwent whatever romantic/religious/inspirational crisis I believe I remember his saying he experienced circa 1961, Iris Murdoch. His book reviews catch the accents of Edmund Wilson and Henry James. In the imaginary interviews I sometimes have with *The Paris Review* I have happily envisioned myself making long heterogeneous lists of predecessors in answer to that inevitable question: I'd say, "My lasting literary influences? Um—*The Tailor of Gloucester*, Harold Nicolson, Richard Pryor, Seuss's *If I Ran the Circus*, Edmund Burke, Nabokov, Boswell, Tintin, Iris Murdoch, Hopkins, Michael Polanyi, Henry and William James, John Candy, *you* know, the usual crowd." But that would be burying Updike deep, and I'm in reaction to Bloom, and therefore can't bury Updike deep the way I might be expected to want to.

There is a confusion here, though. I have been mentioning two separate classes of influence on me as if they were of equivalent weight—Bloom's influence and Updike's influence. One, however, is an influence only on this essay; another is a permanent influence on my life. It thus seems that there are (and I'm sure baby Bloomers have already pointed this out) *contingent* influences and *chronic* influences. A contingent influence springs to mind as you try to solve the problems suggested by a chosen subject and then it goes away: in the case of this essay, in which the subject is a writer thinking about an older writer, the conscious contingent influences that have to be worked around somehow are, in addition to Harold Bloom, Henry James's "The Figure in the Carpet," Frederick Exley's *A Fan's Notes* and *Pages from a Cold Island* (in which he does a lot of thinking about Edmund Wilson), Janet Malcolm's great recent thing about journalistic betrayal, James Atlas's *The Great Pretender*, some diary entries by Louis Simpson (I think) that I read years ago in a literary magazine that traced the ups and downs of his feelings for a Trollope novel he was reading, Proust's *Contre Sainte-Beuve*, Barnes's *Flaubert's Parrot*, and Cyril Connolly's *Enemies of Promise*. This is the arrangement of bayonets and blowguns whose hostage I currently am and whose exact middle point, as far from any single peril of encroachment as possible, is what I'm trying to find as I write; and yet when I'm done, the particular threats will tiptoe off as quickly as they came and I will be surprised to remember, when I see the shape my essay finally takes, how uncomfortable and beset they all made me feel. In recently skimming Exley's *Pages from a Cold Island*, for instance, I worried that his book begins with his reading of the death of Edmund Wilson in the paper, just as this essay begins with my hearing of the death of Barthelme, and I reassured myself by saying, ah, but that is just where *you* are trying to take the next step, since Exley then occupies himself with talking to Edmund Wilson's daughter and rereading his fiction, whereas you leave Barthelme behind and move to someone whose survivors aren't yet hugely important, because the man lives still! And I note, too, that Exley doesn't feel he has to mention Harold Bloom just because he's doing a book about literary influence, and I don't miss his mentioning Harold Bloom, and yet out of some grinding gear of self-betrayal I have to do it: perhaps it's what my grandfather, who wanted very much to be a novelist and patterned his very alcoholism on Fitzgerald's and Norman Douglas's habits, called "the ingrown toenail of the Quaker conscience."

Unlike contingent influences, who (or which) you are always hoping will turn out to be more different from you than you felt them to be at the time they made themselves known, permanent influences like Updike (and, to a lesser extent, Nabokov) make you very unhappy when they threaten to be more unlike you as human beings than you had thought. In some review or address Updike praises the capacity to lie as being of all traits the most important to the novelist. I felt myself disagreeing so violently as I read this that my whole imaginary friendship with Updike was momentarily disrupted: it was, first, a cliché of American writing seminars and book reviews, and it went utterly against what I believed (which was that the urge *not* to lie about, not to be unfair to, not to belie what was there was the dominant propellant, and the desire to undo earlier lies of our own or of others was what drew us on to write further, and that intentional lying came in only at those always dissatisfying points where the futile pursuit of coherence or economy temporarily won out), but more than that, it seemed to go against what Updike had a hundred times shown himself to believe—when for instance he said that comedy was an unsatisfactory form because it forced one to falsify and exaggerate, and when he claimed superbly in the foreward to *Olinger Stories*, "Not an autobiography, they [the stories] have made one impossible" (though it turns out, as I knew it would, that this isn't true—see *Self-Consciousness*), and when he quotes (in a review of *Lectures on Russian Literature*) with surprised and amused neutrality Nabokov's naïve-sounding (but correct) contention that fiction is a gradually evolving effort to be more accurate about life. Because you are matching yourself constantly against a permanent influence, any divergence between you and him assumes the proportions of a small crisis, any convergence is an occasion to nod as if it were all in the cards: when Updike had Henry Bech smugly report (in a pretend interview) that Updike still had all his hair, I thought, What a rotten thing to say—rotten in that it shows such public pride at his exemption from the horror of hair loss, and rotten in that it proves that he and I are different in this crucial respect. When my psoriasis began to get bad, on the other hand, I welcomed its spread at first—I'd been worried that because the disease had shown up late in me (phase I involved only the scalp and penis) and was for five years insignificant compared with Updike's affliction (he had one unfortunate fictional representative *vacuuming out* the bed every morning) I possessed by implication a writing talent less prodigal in its mitotic unstoppableness than Updike's own. Normally if I read something I think is wrong, I forget it two days later (except in unusual cases, like Bloom's burial phrase above); but with Updike, when I disagree with him, there is an element of pain, of emotional rupture, that makes me remember my difference, and as a result I keep returning unhappily to it over the years and checking to see whether the disaccord remains in effect—and because each time I check it I have to find grounds that still satisfy me for my continued refusal to be convinced by what he's said, I am able to refine my opinions in a way I could never do if I did find him universally agreeable. For instance, I often test whether I still disagree with something I read in 1984 in *Hugging the Shore*, standing in what was then called the Paperback Booksmith on Boylston Street in Boston. (I didn't buy the paperback until 1987.) Updike was reviewing one of Wilson's journals, I think. He says that journal-keeping was not the way to write novels—when you wrote novels, you couldn't quarry from journals, you had to let the past bubble up. Naipaul had said something similar, and so had Anthony Powell, but they weren't imaginary friends the way Updike was, so I wasn't concerned by their opinions. But Updike went on to quote a passage from Wilson's journal about a sunset or something [yes—a sunset in Provincetown—I'm amazed I remembered its subject!], and said that it couldn't be used in fiction, that it would "clog any narrative." I fretted, and still fret, over these words. I object to his reviewery certainty here, and I particularly object to his use of the word "clog," which in this context seems deliberately overcolorful and down-homey without being original. There was, as with his statement about lying in fiction, self-rejection in it, since many of his best moments, like Nabokov's, *are* clogs to the narrative: the description of the rain-wetted screen in *Of the Farm*, "like a sampler half-stitched"; and the description of Peggy asleep after the hero's and the mother's long conversation, her shoes "lying beside her feet as if dislodged by a shift of momentum"; and the interior of the gas tank in *The Centaur* [no, *Of the Farm*], and the tire tracks in the snowy parking lot in "A Sense of Shelter" and, best of all, the magnificent passage in which the hero mows the field in *Of the Farm*: a description that carries the burden too of expressing the price you pay for description, as more and more of your life is mowed, and the hopping creatures that are unhoused seek refuge in the odd triangles and rectangles of rough that still remain. What he meant to say, I thought, I hoped, was that Edmund Wilson's passage was simply no good, not that one's aim was to avoid clogging narratives with description. The only thing I *like* are the clogs—and when, late in most novels, there are no more in the pipeline to slow things down, I get that fidgety feeling, and I start bending the pliable remainder of the book so that it makes a popping sound, and I pick off the price sticker on the back and then regret doing so and stick it back on because it is a piece of information I will always want to have (a delight, as Updike memorably says of picking at a psoriasis lesion, thereby capturing a whole world of furtiveness we would otherwise not know about, that "must be experienced to be forgiven"). I wanted my first novel to be a veritable infarct of narrative cloggers; the trick being to feel your way through each clog by blowing it up until its obstructiveness finally revealed not blank mass but unlooked-for seepage-points of passage.

In August, speaking of clogs, while I was thinking about this essay and not writing it, the sewer in my in-laws' house backed up. The service, with the appealing name of Another Rooter, had to be called twice. The problem finally turned out to be tampons: their strings caught on a tufty invading root and expanded to the full extent of their puff, about thirty of them. Earthworms took up residence in them—a bizarre gloss on Andrew Marvell. "I found your problem," the rooter called up nonchalantly, and beckoned me down to an Edenic scene in the lower garden near the standpipe: around the probe of his machine was a roil of roots and black tampon-fruits and pinkly prosperous earthworms. "Best to cut the strings off," he advised, and wrote "sanetery napkens" on the invoice—our vocabulary always lags reality. And why shouldn't this very clog clog some narrative of mine? To the worms it was not obstructive, it wasn't revolting, it was life itself. It is life itself. I'm delighted by the idea that these tampons (which their user treated as Elvis Presley treated his scarves in his decline, barely touching them to his neck before flinging them mechanically out to the audience as souvenirs) underwent this lurid purgatorio out in the garden.

Here again, though, I think I understand what Updike was doing in censuring clogs. When he wrote the review of Edmund Wilson's diary he was tired of the Proustian and Nabokovian and *Of the Farm*ian set piece. He was tired of the feel of cranking up those cylinders in himself. The most fertile internal acres of lyrical observation had already been mowed. Increasingly he was interested in the other things novelists are expected to do. Even the very word "clog" shows his impatience with his old self. After a certain point, the management of one's own past vocabulary, the avoidance of repetition, becomes a major burden. Your earlier formulations become contingent influences—and they hunt you down. An interviewer asked him if he worried in writing so much about repeating himself, and he said something like, You do after a while get the feeling of having been in the same place before. Ah! When I first read that, years ago, I wanted so badly to know that feeling! If, on a dozen earlier narrative occasions, you've *obstructed* the narrative, caused the narrative to *hang fire*, made it *negotiate a trifling embouchement*, etc., you finally get a kick out of using the word that you've been holding at bay all these years: you've earned the privilege of using it—to you it's fresh, since what feels tired now are your own earlier attempts at freshness. The sheer amount of memory it takes as you're writing and you pause at some nominative juncture and review the options, and one by one reject those that file before your mind because you clearly recall or dimly suspect that you've found an earlier home for them—the sheer mounting strain of this, like the strain of a chess player who has to keep every move of every game he has ever played available for immediate review—must be exhausting. (Updike mentions the theme of suburban adultery that has occupied him since *Marry Me*, "a subject that, if I have not exhausted it, has exhausted me." Clever bastard!) It is almost with relief that once in a while we think we have come across a pre-enjoyed image, such as the white crosswalk lines on the street that are pulled this way and that by passing cars in *Of the Farm* and another book. (The image bears up well under this joint custody, by the way [if joint custody it is: I thought the second crosswalk image was in *The Centaur* but I wasn't able to find it there]—though we take to it in part because we feel tender toward it, uncertain of the level of Updike's devotedness: yes, he liked it enough to consent to it when it appeared in a street scene the first time, and yet he didn't like it well enough for his memory to warn him off a second placement.) How many *hundreds* of book reviews has he embarked on—even in the rigidly conventionalized first sentence or two of these exacting études forever finding some tilt or pressure of the needle that allows entrance into that scarred and track-marked territory of literary synopsis, correlation, and judgment? I can feel his pride, despite his expressions of relative coolness toward his nonfictional achievements, when he quietly says in the acknowledgments page for *Hugging the Shore*, that *x* and *y* and *z* first appeared in *The New Yorker*, along with "ninety-two of the book reviews." What an astounding number! You know he's slightly proud of it: there was no reason he had to count them.

At some point, then, at several points, Updike must have felt that panic that the founder of any highly successful entrepreneurial concern feels, when his business has grown so big that he can't remember all of his employees' names. The very sensation of that overfertile sump of your own previous usages, a vast dying sea just on its own, never mind the rest of the marine world, begins to force you in the direction of simplicity: you can see this force operating, for example, in an essay Updike wrote for *Esquire* in 1987, about listening to the radio. (I remember the essay well because, though it didn't say what I wanted to say, it still came too close to an essay I was doing on the same subject for me to finish mine.) In it, Updike remembers how in the cold car of his childhood (the same car as in *The Centaur*), he would "lean into the feeble glow of the radio dial as if into warmth," and he brings his radio affections up to date by saying that he likes a certain tune by Madonna ["True Blue"], and he closes the sentence of approval with a colon and a single word: "catchy." A thirty-year-old Updike would never have resorted to that word, because calling a tune "catchy" isn't on its own interesting enough: the Updike of that era would have exerted himself to find a more refulgent dinglebolly of an adjective as diligently as Whitney Balliet, that tireless prodigy, still does in writing about music. But Updike has chosen "catchy," and it satisfies us in its setting, because he feels and we feel the inversion of word frequency that happens over the course of a life of careful writing, as the near-to-hand and superficially uninteresting become interesting through relative neglect. If you begin as something of a mannerist and phrasemaker, you offer yourself the hope of gradually disgusting yourself into purity and candor; if on the other hand you start by affecting a direct Saxon scrubbedness, then when a decade or so later you are finally ready to cut through the received ideas to say something true, the simplicity will feel used up and hateful and you'll throw yourself with a wail on the OED and bring up great dripping sesquipedalian handfuls while your former admirers shake their chignons in pity. I know perfectly well that I should not be using inkhorners like "florilegia" when I mean "collection" and "plenipotentiary" when I mean "stand-in" at my age (b. 1957)—and though the latinate conscripts were indeed the ones that first sprang to mind as I was typing those sentences, I did look askance at them on the screen a minute after I used them, for two reasons. First, because their eager scholasticism made me wonder if others would wonder whether my choices had leaped from a thesaurus or one of those maddening block calendars that offer a new vocabulary word every day. (I *still* find the deracinated adjacency of the thesaurus objectionable, and never use one, and feel guilty when I try to make a dictionary serve the same slatternly function, and I am only tempted to seek one out in the reference section if I strongly suspect that a reader may say "Florilegia?—right, sure, he just looked up *anthology*, the fraud," and I need to assure myself that the word I used is not sitting right there three words over from the

word I think the reader will sneerily suppose I was wishing
to avoid, and even then I resist the urge, because if I do
find that the word I want to use is there and I avoid it I
will be operating under the influence of Roget's, too. Yet
at the same time I hate all this overscrupulousness and I am
drawn to Updike's honest picture of himself in "Getting the
Words Out" as "paw[ing]" through dictionaries and thesauruses, and I similarly admired Barthelme when at the
Berkeley writers' conference he blew Leonard Michaels's
(pale yellow) socks off by casually saying in a question-and-
answer session that *sure* he used a thesaurus, *absolutely*; I
love both Updike's and Barthelme's implied boredom with
the purist's pretense that every word he uses has to have
been naturally retrieved from a past passage. So I agree with
Updike that a thesaurus isn't intrinsically evil, and yet I can't
use one—and I even feel slightly guilty when I use a certain
word whose placement I have admired in something by
Updike in roughly the same way he uses it: for instance, I
wrote the phrase "consorted in the near vestibules of my
attention" in my second novel, and I used "consorted" because one morning I was reading a review of a novel (can't
remember which one) in *Hugging the Shore* and was struck
by a lovely use of "consort" ["... better consorts with our
sense of what a writer should be ..." in a review of Beckett's
Mercier and Camier] and again worried, just as I had all
those years ago when I read "absurdly shook my head No"

that I would never write as well as Updike. But now that I know from *Self-Consciousness* that Updike regularly uses thesauruses, I'm drawn to show the same dismissiveness toward "consort" that I worry others will direct at my use of "florilegia": it ("consort" I mean) now feels as if he found it under "adjacency" or some other big rubric, when honestly he could have found it in a thousand places—Henry James is a frequent consorter, for example.) And, second, I looked askance at "florilegia" and "plenipotentiary" because I felt a needle jump in my déjà vu-meter that might indicate that I'd used them both before, and I didn't like the idea of people (i.e., Updike) thinking, "Florilegia *again*? It wasn't that great the first time! He's pretending his vocabulary is a touch-me-anywhere-and-I'll-secrete-a-mot-juste kind of thing, when it turns out to be this cribbed little circle of favored freaks that he uses over and over hoping nobody will notice!" So what I have to do now is to search the disks that hold my two novels for the words "florilegia" and "plenipotentiary"—an activity that has to be as artificial as any thesaurus search. Each novel I write will introduce another layer of this vocabularistic panic, and increasingly I will come to recognize the utility of words and phrases that don't make waves, since their very commonness keeps them from being noted as events that can or cannot be unintentionally repeated; and eventually, one morning when I'm fifty or so, I will be trying to work up my long-abandoned notes for a pop music essay, and I'll want simply to say that a certain song is good, and the adjectives will line up for the casting session, and one by one I will nod as they twirl past in the half-lit stage, saying I used you, too old, too young, I used you, I used you, I didn't use you for x reason, I didn't use you for y reason, and finally, like Hope following all the evils that flap out of Pandora's box, the word "catchy" will flutter up, "Like a virgin, touched for the very first time," as Madonna would say, and I will think, Hey!—but then, because I quoted it to illustrate the whole problem of vocabulary management in this essay, I will remember that Updike already used it and that it is off-limits, and, in a wistful non sequitur, I will find myself wishing that I had been Updike's friend. Catchy, catchy: it *is* a beautiful word.

But I don't mean of course to suggest that Updike's developmental path has taken him from obscure latinity to Saxon simplicity: from the first he has been a sultan of the monosyllable, and of the monosyllabic settings for richesse, as when in *Of the Farm* he mentions "the pool of a dandelion," using "pool" here, I think, to mean the whitish spherical frizz of Tinkertoyed seeds, a botanical sense of the word that is interestingly unfamiliar to me, or when in one of his early poems he talks about the view from shipboard:

> The blue below
> Is Aquamarine
> Sometimes the blue below
> Is green

[The real lines, from "Shipbored," are:

> That line is the horizon line.
> The blue above it is divine.
> The blue below it is marine.
> Sometimes the blue below is green.]

The comic movement of the stanza turns on the opposition [in my garbled and impoverished version, not in Updike's real version] between the line-filling latinity of "aquamarine" humbled into the contradictory surprise of "green." But the best example of this sort of syllabic eloquence that I can remember is near the end of the introduction to *Hugging the Shore*, when, after complaining about the dangers of writing book reviews, he says that the money he got from writing them "roughly balanced a monthly alimony payment that was mine to make." "Mine to make" is awfully good: a state of penance conveyed by the King Jamesian ring of duties as privileges; a whole bible of contrition "foreshortened" (as King Henry James would say) into a single cadence. Nabokov may have been showily able to describe dog urine in snow as "xanthic holes," but he was not enough of a native speaker to get the mine-to-make kind of melody.

No, the confusion of verbal oddity with exuberance, and of neologism (especially noun/adjective and adjective/noun transvestitism) with strength of conviction, is my problem, not Updike's. I want *not* to use "florilegia" but I can't help myself. I'm afraid of small pure words like "sky" or "water" or "blue" or "green": they too quickly induce an auto-suggestive trance of consent and submission, in which (as with "catchy" above) you say, "Ah, simple, beautiful, beautiful, simple!"; and in less than fifteen seconds that isolated vocable has expanded to blot out everything else—all intelligence, all conscience, all conversation, all libraries—

sky

And it's too much! You lose your bearings! Every concrete substantive seems arbitrarily lyrical! You don't need paragraphs or arguments or careful description at all! To protect yourself from this agoraphobic sensation of falling into a bottomless and eventually toxic word, you need a clunkier and uglier and more conspicuously Victorian vocabulary around it, full of *nearly*s and *indeed*s and *even*s and *himself*s—terms of near but not perfect transparency, that can almost be employed every fifth sentence or so without anyone's noticing, but not quite—so that you can *use* the language freely, without being transfixed into a mute and foolish nounage by the sacredness of the words you learned first.

6

As I feared, *sky* has sucked me in. For I had planned, in bringing the last paragraph to a close and in opening up this one, to say that I had a good deal more to say about the whole problem of self-repetition and self-influence (a problem which we can be sure that Updike takes seriously, since in a review of a late Borges collection he points out that the blind belletrist quotes the same passage from Chesterton in three separate places), but that my wife gave me Thomas Mallon's brand-new *Stolen Words* for Christmas (yes, it is already December 28, 1989, and I have only gotten this far in this essay!), which includes (p. 140) a brief discussion of the topic of self-repetition that though incomplete neutralized my own parochial sense of novelty; moreover (I planned to say) I was beginning to comprehend, by extending Updike's notion of novelistic space into the wider dimension of *oeuvral* space, that not everything I had mounded up to say under a given head needed to be said in one spot: I could leave some images or observations

unshoehorned and trust that they would clamor their unexpected pertinence later on; later on in the same essay or
book, or later on in a different essay or book—although I
was also beginning to see that by putting aside some of what
you had to say for later (out of simple consideration for the
reader's already redlining threshold of vexation and puzzlement, and out of the desire to demonstrate that you were
not so compulsive that you couldn't avoid narrative clogs
when you wished to), you condemned yourself to the appearance of another sort of compulsion, in that readers
would be sure to assume that your later returns to the subject
came about because you were *drawn inexorably* toward a
certain theme, when in truth you would have been delighted
never to have to mention it again if there had been any
reasonably graceful way to include all of it in one extended
shishkebob. For instance (I planned to point out) in writing
my second novel I had found that I had more to say about
model airplanes and about coins than I could possibly ac-
commodate on its already overburdened chassis: I was distressed to see this; I had to keep telling myself that there
would be other occasions—and indeed I found a way to
clean out the entire model airplane depository in the essay
I wrote just before starting on this piece of madness about
Updike, and in this very thing on Updike I have successfully
gotten rid of one of the coin sequences left over from the
novel. But at a price: I now will seem to be obsessed with

model airplanes and coins, when on my scale of obsessions they are very low. (Even to call Updike an obsession—my wife first used the word on me in this connection in 1987—overstates it; for though I think about Updike a lot I seldom read him: surely a true obsessive would read all the available works.)

More disheartening still, in finding a stable environment for the last coin sequence (me at McDonald's reading James after the five hundred pennies) I find that I also offer the reader the opportunity to accuse me of being overinterested in scenes in which a person *eats and thinks* at the same time: my first book describes a thoughtful lunch hour, and my second is about a man giving a bottle to an infant while again thinking away, and now I have a guy (really and truly me this time, though only a tiny transverse slice of me) chewing on a Big Mac and reading about James's stream of thought. I don't want my work to have this prominent "philosophical snack" motif! And yet the repetition of this type of moment was unavoidable: I had to balance the relief of consigning a large scoop of my residual coin-moments to this essay (there is, happily, only one more large scoop to go) against the possible career harm of seeming to imply by this recurrence that I want above all to be remembered in the act of chewing. Relief won in this case. But I am at a very delicate point in my development, it now occurs to me: the point where you decide that some thematic repetitions aren't going to be thought of as unwelcome evidence of a failure to strike out in new directions but as lifelong themes: like the "Nina"s hidden in every Hirschfeld, or the moths and fritillaries that come back in Nabokov, or Updike's sweetly graphic sexual infidelities, or Melville's sea. The question is, is eating-and-thinking going to be my "Nina" or not? I hope not.

So I meant to go on to say this about repetition, treating it slightly more fully than I have been able to in renouncing my intention to treat it, but that word "sky" has unexpectedly stopped the forward flow of my essay: not exactly with the lethal bottomlessness of the simple concrete word, but with that more general hypertrophied word and phrase reverence that has much to do with flash cards, and which has proven to be, in fact, one of the worst hazards of the sort of criticism of Updike I'm engaged in here, a style of book chat that, in the unlikely event that it has not already been recognized and does not already have a name, might be called something sexy like *memory criticism*, or *phrase filtration*, or *closed book examination*. If it is merely a subset of the "reader response" school (which I know nothing about), or is a variant of the old Paterian impressionistic criticism or of Arnold's touchstone technique, fine—but if it is something new, I'm raising my flag now! Nobody can take this supreme moment from me, if it is a moment! ("Too clever by half" is a charge I've never understood. Who originated it and why has its unambitious ratio persisted to damn so effortlessly all of our wildest upsurges?) Leave aside the other strains in this essay, such as the interleaving of autobiography (familiar enough, perhaps), and the insistence that what I'm doing be done on a living writer: memory criticism, understood as a form of commentary that relies entirely on what has survived in a reader's mind from a particular writer over at least ten years of spotty perusal, is possibly a new and useful way of discussing literature. Its risks are (1) that it depends to an unusual extent on whether you like me and whether consequently you have some faith that even though I may remember an entirely different set of phrases from Updike than you remember, you feel that you could conceivably have remembered them yourself, had you read what I had read by Updike in the order I read it, and were Updike as important to you as he apparently is to me. And (2) if it is indeed a new style of interpretation, it promises to open a depressing flood of bad work that strings together a couple of three-word phrases by a certain writer and a few "Well, *I* remember"s. And (3) this abuse will in time bring about another deadly wave of close reading in reaction, for of course instead of pulling you back to the books under discussion, this approach pulls you away from them, demanding that you not consult them while you are letting your thoughts clarify. And (4) it assumes that the filtration processes of memory are less chancy, more dependably self-consistent, than they really are. Those are the risks. But it is a lot of fun, and it offers a nice pseudoscientific thrill as you begin to treat your haphazard book-memories as a fund of data on which to operate, and it costs nothing, takes no great reading, and forces a degree of honesty from the critic that might, for about five minutes, be beneficial. But no, no—I don't want it to happen: the fame that comes from having touched off or reinforced some humanistic trend, and especially from having supplied a phrase that too succinctly sums up the whole approach, is not the kind of slow-burn fame that a novelist needs to keep developing. Manifesto-fame kills. I don't *want* to see the techniques of "closed book examination" applied to any other novelist. I want this essay to be the end of it. I hate myself for trying even jokingly to increase its market penetration with a cheap name. It reminds me of Gilbert Ryle's employment of the term "category mistake" in debunking the existence of mental entities—the phrase was too powerful for its own good, it fell into the wrong hands, spread too quickly, destroyed any helpfulness it may at first have helped disseminate. Sexy names are so often Germanic noun pairs or trios: *category mistake, paradigm shift, catastrophe theory, reader response criticism*. And now something like *deprived recall analysis*? No! Fight it off. When a snippet like "vast dying sea" sticks in your memory even when shorn of its casings, this durability is a good thing, because the phrase is intrinsically interesting and funny—the foundling survives on its own merits, not on its promise. "Paradigm shift," on the other hand, never moved anyone to tears (and I will instantly admit that it is a good deal snappier, more catchy, than my own attempted catchphrases): it was *all* promise, it offered the prospect of infinite applicability, of normally reticent colleagues from a hundred distinct disciplines singing in one great lusty chorus. The fate of "paradigm shift" rises or falls with every subtle or crude application of the theory it stands for; whereas "vast dying sea" is self-reliant, and it can only be harmed by my unrelenting overquotation. But if I were an American academic, I don't think I would be able to resist turning my memory-filtered approach to Updike into a method. I would check hurriedly to be sure that Walter Benjamin or one of the Frenchmen hadn't done it all already, and if it looked as if it was indeed sufficiently new, I would sketch out a first footnote that found hints of my new approach in Updike himself, when he says that Eliot's plays fade, "as most plays do," but lines of his poetry have a grim ability to hang on [". . . what lines of poetry between Yeats's late poems and the verse that Roethke and Sylvia Plath wrote from within the shadow of death burn deeper, better remember themselves, than Eliot's?"]; and in Henry James, when in the midst of his Hawthorne study he offers an account of how as a boy he first heard the title *The Scarlet Letter* and felt its power, and how later at a museum someone pointed out a painting on the subject of *The Scarlet Letter* to him and told him it was about a book he would someday read, and how he first read the opening pages of a middle installment of *Madame Bovary: Etude des moeurs* near a fire-place in Paris as a teenager and felt the pull of its title and its style before it was dignified by the salvers of fame; and in George Saintsbury, when he worried that he hadn't noticed lately the incidental quotations and passing mentions of Smollett which in the world of letters are the principal means we have of knowing the degree of a writer's "sempervirescence"; and in Anthony Burgess when he praised scenes in Isherwood's *A Single Man* for their surprising ability to stay with you; and in Frost, in his potsticker about the poet's task being to come up with words that "lodge" in the memory—and I would find some other obscurer examples that felt apt and toss them in and perhaps scramble the order so that Updike and James weren't once again at the top, and I'd say—ah, they all had inklings, they all felt instinctively that the closed book examination of literature was of primary importance, but none of them thought to make it a method. That's what I might say. But I'm not an American academic. (Harvard's philosophy department rejected my application for graduate study in 1981—and why? Because I'd taken only three philosophy courses in college, two of these during my freshman year in music school? Because I'd gotten a trilobitic score on the Logic and Reasoning section of the GRE trivium? Because my application essay was ten pages of pompous pleading that ended by my misspelling and misusing the word "elenchus"? These aren't *reasons*.) I count myself fortunate in being able to extract all the pretend-scholarly pleasure I want out of my method without urging it on anyone else.

In fact, at this very moment I have at my left elbow a rubber-banded pile of three-by-five cards, each holding a phrase I remember from Updike, sorted in alphabetical order by key word. I'm modeling myself on Nabokov's lovable Pnin, who retires to a carrel with one drawer of the card catalog like a squirrel with a nut—and on Nabokov himself, of course, who detailed his three-by-five-card method of fictional composition so comprehensively that Gore Vidal said in some essay that he was sick of hearing about it. I have only to pluck out one of these phrase cards at random, such as *presided over by a serene and mutual deafness*, Updike's perfect characterization of Nabokov's and Wilson's epistolary argument over poetic meter, to feel that I have dots left to connect, and that I am crisply advancing the cause of self-knowledge. [The correct quotation, however, is "derived from a serene and mutual deafness."] But when I came to the end of that earlier paragraph, with the vastness of the open sky visible through a rent in it, I thumbed through these three-by-five cards in vain: I found I had no simple way back to Updike. I could mention an aerial description

I knew from *Marry Me* that goes (in my misremembered version)

> Sally became a bird, a heroine. The clouds boiled beneath her, radiant, motionless. For twenty pages of Camus, while the air conditioner nozzle whispered in her hair, something something something

[and in Updike's real version:

> Then Sally flew; she became a bird, a heroine. She took the sky on her back, levelled out on the cloudless prairie above the clouds—boiling, radiant, motionless—and held her breath for twenty pages of Camus while the air-conditioner nozzle whispered into her hair.]

which I remember simply because I was distressed in 1987 to come across the throwaway mention of the air nozzle in Updike after I had resolved to write in detail about my own reverence for it. (The only other mention I knew of was in John Dickson Carr's 1951 *The Nine Wrong Answers*, in which it's called a "little ventilator" that sends "a shaft of cool air on [the hero's] face.") But this sky-*Marry Me* connection led me nowhere useful. Or I could make an imperious sort of modern transition by first citing Updike's mention of something that John Hawkes had once told him, which was (approximately), "When I want a character to fly, I just say, 'He flew' " (see, I would never have taken this piece of advice to heart if Hawkes himself had said it to me, because Hawkes's fictional imagery is too gruesome for him to be a possible friend, but transmitted through Updike I have found it very useful), and by then announcing that I was adapting Hawkes via Updike by saying "When I want to make a transition, I just say, 'I'm making a transition' "— but again there was no promise of riches beyond the pass. Or I could simply rattle on about influence, but I felt that I badly needed a break from that.

So I was left with the word "sky"—and as everything I had still to say crowded tighter around this sudden hole in my essay, shouting advice and pointing urgently off in different directions, I began to notice that the sensation of tumbling into a word like "sky" was not much different from the sensation I had experienced already several times in thinking over one or another of Updike's phrases: set off on three-by-five cards, they now constituted my universe, or rather my dictionary, and consequently each was prone to an alarming inflation. On one card I have a slightly garbled version of Updike's *Picked-Up Pieces* politesse toward his fact checkers: "Many the untruth quietly curbed, the misspelling invisibly mended." *Quietly curbed*—simple, beautiful, beautiful, simple! I have reduced Updike's millions of words to these few flash cards, and like the disembodied idioms that are projected behind Talking Heads in *Stop Making Sense*, the isolates I have rubber-banded together can rapidly become too incantatory to retain their standing as exemplars of grace.

But I can always stop flipping through them; I can always leave the rubber band undisturbed: really it is only the physical availability of the three-by-five stack, the fact of it at my elbow, that I need, since it sustains the temporarily pleasurable illusion that I am a graduate student in some delightfully narrow (but fully accredited) course of study and research. As a matter of fact, on the night I first thought of rationalizing my Updike memories on file cards (December 5, 1989), I had an unusually complete dream in which I enrolled in a high-powered Melville seminar at a prestigious university. I caught a glimpse of some of the other seminar participants on registration day: they were all young women, likable-seeming, plain, disturbingly intelligent and well read. I hurried to the dream's bookstore because I knew almost nothing about Melville and feared humiliation, and I found there a slipcased edition of a slim green and black biography of the author by V. S. Pritchett that I was amazed to see was part of the long-defunct "English Men of Letters" series. Opening it, I thought I saw a copyright date of 1888, but giving it a moment's thought, I knew I must have misread the century, since Pritchett is still alive, and for him to have written such a book in 1888 would make him at least a hundred and twenty years old now. I pulled it out of the slipcase and opened it; I came to a page that was very thick, like those pretend books you can buy from Barnes & Noble whose interiors have a big hole cut in them to store valuables: there was a printed warning saying "Punch Bound," and I realized that I was looking at something very similar to the back of a pop-up or "turn and learn" children's book page, where the rivets and tabs and sliding mechanisms of the understructure are fully disclosed. As I began to turn this resistant page, I saw a soft white whale-tail begin to emerge, made from a three-quarter-inch pile of Kleenexes cut into a tail shape; when I opened further, the rest of the bias-folded cetacean, made out of the same thickness of brand-new Kleenex, rose out of the book and straightened itself out. It seemed odd that the young Pritchett would have felt it necessary to resort to a *pop-up* to demonstrate what a white whale looked like, but I nonetheless admired the oddity, and I thought that the book, though expensive (thirty-nine dollars), would appreciate dramatically in value because of this feature. I decided I had to buy it: the promise of Pritchett's careful, unbaroque prose applied to a sloppy but brilliant American like Melville was very exciting, and its lack of critical jargon would serve as a useful corrective to the Melville seminar, filled with supersmart grad students who had read ten times what I had read. I had some trouble getting the Kleenex whale to fold away properly back into the book, and I felt once again the familiar sadness about display items, which in abetting the sale of identical but sealed versions of themselves are treated so carelessly by shoppers that they will never find a buyer of their own, and as a result I decided that I would *not* put the demo edition back on the shelf and buy the unopened one, but would buy instead this very one I had already fingered, despite the crumpled tail. How exciting it was to be beginning an English seminar after all these years, and after all the scorn I'd felt toward the academic study of literature! And how exciting that all the smart grad students would have read the latest American biography, while I would have the principal events of Melville's life funneled through old Pritchett's natty English mind! As I turned toward the cash register, I woke, feeling for once that the term "well rested" had meaning. And that morning, still under the grad-student spell, I located in my office an unopened packet of three-by-five cards that I'd bought several years earlier, having seen them in a stationery store and thought, I'll never use these guys, but I have to own them anyway. When I was twelve, I saw my mother use a green metal box filled with three-by-five cards in connection with some course she was taking for her master's degree, and when my sixth-grade teacher told my reading group that we ought to start "building" our vocabularies by writing the definitions of unfamiliar words down as we came across them, I asked my mother for a similar green box and some cards of my own, which she bought for me. I placed the box on top of my desk at school with the clean sense of starting out on a project: coin collecting had lasted two weeks as a hobby, model-airplane building had lasted two years—but now, in word collecting, I thought (mistakenly) that I had found something superior, more permanent, than either of these. For several days I carried the green box back and forth on the school bus, in case I came across a notable word at home, but it was awkward to hold, and I was finding anyway that I was fussy about what words I wanted it to contain. So far the only ones that had seemed worthy of the box were "aesthetic" and "antidisestablishmentarianism," and the latter I wrote down reluctantly, because it was such a hackneyed longie. I told my father about my new hobby, and I asked him if *he* knew any interesting words. I was eating an orange, I think. He said, "Sure! You're starting with *a*? All right. Here's a word that sounds like *aesthetic: ascetic*. You know that one?"

"I think I do," I said. But I didn't.

"*Ascetic* means *self-denying*. You forgo pleasures. And then there's a word that sounds like *ascetic*, which is *acidic*." That one was too easy; I wrote it down to humor him anyway. I didn't want more. But he was on a roll. "And there's one other, that sounds like *acidic*—there's one other you might find interesting," he said. He told me one more word. Occasionally, years afterward, I would picture this long-lost green hinged box (it sat on my desk that whole school year

but my vision of its being packed with well-thumbed vocabulary cards never materialized—the cards stayed blank;
I added almost nothing to it after my father's contributions)
and I would recall my father giving me that graduated series
of near homonyms, and I would try to resurrect what the
last word had been. Hassidic? Asymptotic? Once you decide
on a profession, you riffle back through your past to find
early random indications of a leaning toward your chosen
interest and you nurture them into a false prominence: so
it was naturally very important to me, as a writer on the
make, to have this sixth-grade vocabularistic memory in its
complete form. It was still incomplete, however, when on
December 5 I found the unopened, plastic-covered packet
of Oxford Index Cards ("100 Cards, 8 pt. Standard Grade,
manufactured and distributed by Esselte Pendaflex Corpo-
ration, Made in USA, Item no. 31") and began, with an
immoderate sixth-grader's delight, to copy down my store
of remembered Updikean phrases. Above the single candy-
stripe of the magenta line I wrote down the quotation, as
well as I remembered it; below, on the blue pin-striping,
was the source, if I knew it, and the date and time I made
the card, and what number it was in the total sequence, and
any other notes I felt called on to make. I saw myself sorting
this deck in tricky ways; shuffling it repeatedly to attain a
veracious stochasticism; checking individual cards off in several colors and with several attractively cryptic check marks

(green circled x's, little blue spirals, long and short arrows to indicate linkages with other cards); flipping through them at high speed in spare moments, like a language student studying for a final; laying them all out side by side on the rug and playing some sort of game of concentration with them. I very much wanted them to become dog-eared. I wanted to get good at wristily doubling the rubber band around them when I had finished with them for the day. But I half knew at the outset that they would prove less useful than the initial pleasure of filling them out would lead me to expect—and in truth they haven't been helpful, except, as I say, as a physical presence. Many of the quotations I use here I didn't write down on cards, and many of the ones I did write down on cards I didn't find a place for.

But never mind! That very day, December 5, after blowing most of the morning making out cards and rereading what I'd written of the whole essay up to that point, I was finally able, with Updike's help, to complete the memory of my father's three vocabulary words. Here's how it happened. I stood in front of the microwave in the kitchen in a state of growing disappointment and self-doubt, sure that this essay was a failure. It was much too long, for one thing. The editor of *The Atlantic* had agreed to a length of seven to ten thousand words, and he had warned me specifically that if I sent them something of twenty or thirty thousand words they just wouldn't know what to do with it. "A long piece eats up so much space in the magazine," he said. "And if it's on a subject that a reader isn't interested in, he thinks he's gotten gypped for that whole month." Gypping the reader? I certainly didn't want to be a party to that! So probably *The Atlantic* would turn it down. Nobly I would refuse the kill fee, since I had not upheld my end of the bargain. Or maybe I couldn't afford to be that noble. I would undoubtedly sink into a severe depression. I had to have a fall-back plan. I might try to persuade a book publisher to bring "U and I" out along with the model airplane essay and the three quasi-philosophical essays that appeared in *The Atlantic* in '82, '83, and '84, as long as I could put some disclaimer in the table of contents that the three philosophical essays were *vehehehery* early work ("Three Early Essays" perhaps, with their dates of publication in parenthesized italics at the end of each, as in Updike's *Museums and Women*, and my birth date screechingly conspicuous in the author's note on the jacket?), or if "U and I"'s path from A to Z wavered and looped for long enough, I could see whether a publisher might bring it out on its own as one of those books that even Gesualdo-tape-playing bookstores don't have a satisfactorily standardized set of shelves for: "Essays and Belles Lettres," or "Criticism," or "Biography." [The editor of *The Atlantic* read the finished essay in February 1990 and called me. "I have the authority to run a piece this long," he said. "But that's like saying that the captain of a Pan Am 747 has the authority to take his family up for a quick flight." A month later he sent me a set of galleys that expertly condensed the essay from forty-five thousand words to thirteen thousand while preserving its general shape. I called him from a pay phone near my dermatologist, nauseous and glum from PUVA therapy pills, and said no: seamless though his version was, most of the things that had made the essay seem worth writing were now gone or uncomfortably contiguous. So we agreed instead that *The Atlantic* would publish a fifteen-hundred-word fragment, a solution I liked because that way I would not have to refuse directly the overgenerous kill fee for the original essay and thereby get into a disagreement with my agent, who said I simply could not refuse a kill fee—"Everyone will laugh at you if you do," a disturbing prospect—and the editor wouldn't have to insist in his courtly way on my taking the kill fee, and my relationship with *The Atlantic* would be shakily preserved. But *why* hadn't I been good enough to hijack that transatlantic 747? Why hadn't they run it all, made an exception for me and me only—just as *The New Yorker* made an exception for Barthelme by running all of *Snow White* in one issue?]

Length wasn't the essay's only problem, of course. There was the disturbing question of tone. Beckett's early short disquisition on Proust had come to mind several times as I wrote (I had looked it up in July or August in a different context and read snatches of it), and now I wondered whether the oddly smartass tone I took in places here might share its quality of unease with Beckett's book—an unease that arose from intense, rivalrous, touchy admiration combined with an impatience with criticism as a literary form. Updike himself, I recalled, had in an essay neatly maneuvered past Beckett's exegesis of Proust: "rather acerb," he'd called it. (The same essay on Proust, by the way, contains one of my favorite things in all Updike, when he mentions that a page or two of his copy of Moncrieff's translation is stained with drops of his now-alimonied wife's suntan oil: suntan oil, the thicker exstillation of summer and leisure, crushed from the Palm at the End of the Mind—and I wonder, is this Stevensian sense of "palm" the explanation for why Updike mysteriously changed the title of one of his best early stories from "Walter Briggs" to the less good "Walter Palm" in an eighties trade paperback reissue?—has a Proustian viscosity, I think; I envision the near transparency that the drops of lotion must have created in the paper as methylparaben portholes in Marcel's prose through which we glimpse for a moment the knowable, verifiable life we have now, in America, with spouses and deck chairs and healing sunlight, as opposed to the unknowable life of a homosexual genius in France before the First World War.) And then two neural power lines crossed and I felt a buzz of shorting circuits, for *acerbic* was the very long-lost vocabulary word my father had given me: aesthetic, ascetic, acidic, acerbic.

The sherbety pucker of "acerbic" makes it a better word in some sentences than the more neutrally spirited "acidic"— I saw that; but once my spike of intense joy in having finally remembered the contents of my sixth-grade vocabulary box passed, what interested me was that Updike had used the elegantly curtailed version of the word: *acerb*. This is so like him, to prefer words like "acerb" and "curbed" that enfold more mental syllables than they metrically exhibit. I naturally can't check the date because it would mean opening *Picked-Up Pieces*, but I would suspect that Updike's use of "acerb" in that sentence was roughly contemporaneous (give or take a year) with my father's suggestion of "acerbic" to the sixth-grade me. (The conjunction is coincidental, however: my father is not an Updike reader.) And this sort of timeline matching is, for me at least, one of the basic activities that accompany the admiration of writers of the generation immediately preceding my own: I allow myself to move back from the burbling coffee maker of the present instant along those many linked extension cords of personal identity (rustling twenty-five-foot industrial orange lengths that hurt when you step on them in bare feet, with heavy three-pronged ends; narrower-gauge, permanently kinked white or brown varieties, molded from a cheaper sort of plastic, with a faceted multiple receiving end like a burnt-out brownstone that stolidly resists the intrusion of the average plug) that lead down to the basement of my simpleminded younger self, back to when I sent off coupons to Charles Atlas from the back of comic books and drew plans of the triangular house-on-wheels I was going to live in (with its tiny kitchen and bedroom/driver's seat at the forward apex, and the huge chemistry lab occupying all the rest); and then into the surplus sockets along this jury-rigged linear continuity I plug in one by one the flashing dates and titles of masterpieces from those years—*Revolutionary Road, Of the Farm, A Severed Head, A Single Man*, etc.; and once they are all lit up in Vegas colors, it seems miraculous that I could have lived through that same stretch the first time and not seen or felt any of this buzzing signage. Perhaps you never get over the futile hope that you might be able to rewire your earlier unknowing self so that it was linked from the first to all of those high-voltage parallelisms. Of the relatively few written notes I have made about Updike, the earliest one I've been able to find (written when I was twenty-five in the third person, partly inspired by the Updike story ["Flight"] about the self-conscious seventeen-year-old kid who "went around thinking about [himself] in the third person") attempts this very rewiring. I reproduce it exactly here, misuse of "comprise" and all, with one clarification enclosed in brackets:

6/21/82. Harold, reading Updike's The Centaur, fell in love with the short stOry that comprised chapter two —he thought of 1963, when the book appeared: the nostalgia for Updike's feelings, at the beginnings of his career, mixed with his own early memories of the house they moved to, his family, in 1963—he remembered sitting on the bathroom floor upstairs, looking through a Metropolitan Museum calendar (one of his mother's aunts sent one every year); the numbers 1963 had impressed him then: the specific location in such a wash of millenia—he was sitting with his mouth pressed on his knee, which had an odd taste; now he was so unflexible he had not tasted his knee for over a decade— a datable memory, a memory of the revelation of date, almost as if that moment marked a Piagetian phase. Yet the interesting thing was the connection of this memory with Updike's own reliving of his childhood memories, and the ache of wanting to have been him in 1963, and to equal him now—yet knowing that he [that is, Updike] was at twenty five far more polished than Harold was; and this sadness mixed with the comparison between Updike's mother in Chapter two, and as she appears in the other stories ("Flight"), with his own— the very similar relationship, yet the sense that while Updike was at twenty five fulfilling his special destiny, satisfying the pride of his parents with story after story, Harold's own path was on a steeper, rockier slope—he felt himself, month after month, defining himself on the losing side of the comparison.

The general whimperiness of this passage of mine, combined with the reliance on B-list metaphors like "wash of millenia" [*sic*] and "ache" to keep the prose at a higher verbal pitch than its ideas can hold by themselves, has the ring of vulgarized early Updike, whose boy-heroes are sometimes more sensitive and queasier-stomached than one wants them to

be. You feel when one of his young men's GI-tracts yet
again does some unbecoming acrobatic in reaction to a piece
of social unhappiness that a writing teacher at Harvard must
have told him that it was a good idea to have the reader get
his mood-information through all of his senses, and that
dutifully he is applying this distorting dictum to excess; just
as in movie after movie whenever the character gets a piece
of terrible news the scriptwriter immediately has him or her
bend at the waist, grasp the front bumper, and (to use an
idiom that understandably caught Edmund Wilson's ear)
"snap lunch"—in laziness resorting to brutally externalized
physiology because any subtler sort of core dump is so difficult, cinematically and fictionally, to achieve; and yet hardly
do I venture this small criticism when I remember a later
character, in "Twin Beds in Rome," I think, who much more
believably than his predecessors gets sick on a maritally crucial vacation and can feel in the initial moment of his illness
the entire shape of his stomach within him, *an unprepossessing
tuber*—a magnificent trope, which uses an ugly, earthen,
marginally-edible-sounding thing to describe the location of
the discomfort it would cause if eaten, and which may owe
its existence entirely to the whole unsatisfactory preceding
series of youthful indigestions. [To my astonishment, I have
not found "tuber" so used in "Twin Beds in Rome" or
anywhere else I looked; could it be that I made it up? That
it is my own image? Doubtful. In any case, the passing

sickness in that story works in a way that the bellyaching in *The Centaur* does not.] "To the stomach quatted with dainties," said Lyly, "all trifles seem queasie"; and the moral we might draw from Updike's early prose is that the perfectly healthy, euphuistic wish to caramelize every crab apple and clove every ham ought not to be accompanied by too keen an interest in the hero's emotio-gastric status. (I write this, needless to say, during the holidays.)

But here again, here again, I have to call attention to this problem of tone. Is it like me to rope somebody like John Lyly into the present context? No, it is not. Or rather, it *is* only when I can then call the reference immediately into question by a follow-up act of self-reproach. When Beckett allowed his nervousness about Proust to commandeer his attitude, it made him "acerb," as Updike duly saw; but when I am betrayed by what I take to be a somewhat similar nervousness—a feeling that the stakes are very high, that everything depends on the quality of my thinking right here, that this essay is the test of whether I should bother to be a writer or not, and yet the feeling at the same time that there is a fatal prematurity in so arranging things, since it forces discipleship and competitiveness to clash awkwardly when with time the two would have arrived at a subtler and more composed relationship—the betrayal takes the form of smirks and smartass falsifications, such as when I spoke earlier of trying to "hustle" Updike on the golf course into thinking I was less perceptive than I was, or when I used faux-naïf expletives like "Jeezamarooni!" or called myself a writer "on the make." I really must read *The Anxiety of Influence* as soon as I finish writing this, because the fragmentary idea I have of it keeps steering my approach into oversimplifications. It might even be that two of Updike's own early characters are in large part to blame for my errantly cocky tone—the convergence of contingent and chronic influences being especially hard to shake off. In the story called "The Kid's Whistling" a kid disturbs the creative concentration of a retail-store manager by whistling blithely while the increasingly irritated manager tries to finish a sign that says something like "Have a Happy Holiday" ["Toyland" actually] in multicolored tinsel on glue ["Silverdust" on poster paint]. (I reread this story in 1987, ten years after I first read it, remembering only the title, because I needed to be sure that I wasn't overlapping Updike's use of whistling in a scene in my first novel. Such checking to control against overlaps is in my experience one of the main motives for the miscellaneous reading that writers do.) And in another early story, which I read circa 1978 and whose title I can't bring back ["Intercession"], an overcheerful buttinsky kid messes up the golf game of a somewhat older, more serious sportsman by his running commentary. The Bugs Bunny/ Elmer Fudd pattern of both stories, though it unquestionably does capture a fractional component of the true nature of my feelings toward Updike, is much too easy to ride out into exaggeration—and I am aware too that people would probably rather hear me be smartass, thereby digging my own grave and taking old Updike down a peg or two at the same time, than hear me be grateful and woozily admiring.

And to the extent that my cockiness is useful to Updike himself—as the whistling turns out to be an essential distraction to the retail manager in the first story, and as the buttinsky golf-kid finally helps the elder golfer in the second story to some more distant green of philosophy that I do not remember—I am pleased to carry on with it, but I have been unusually on guard against this fault lately because of something that happened just this September. I was sent a copy of a review of an Iris Murdoch novel that began extremely unusually by saying, "The arrival of this blockbuster [Murdoch's *The Message to the Planet*] interrupted my reading of—" and then mentioned *my first novel*. The reviewer, who was Jan Morris, held Murdoch and me in explicit opposition: to her I represented up-to-the-minutiae, as it were, while Murdoch stood for a tradition that had been played out and ought to be brought to a close. I have had a literary crush on Murdoch since 1985, so I shot off a letter to her saying how horrified I was by the opening gambit of the review and told her that I thought she was the best novelist we have. (I was telling the truth: Updike is my favorite living *writer*; Murdoch is my favorite living *novelist*—although in drawing this distinction I clearly remember how little I liked reading an essay by John Leonard, I think, in *The New York Times Book Review* in 1978 or so in which he named Updike as one of the five best living American writers but then nastily qualified this by saying that Updike was a better essayist than he was a novelist. It doesn't work that way: the novels and essays lend reciprocal authority to one another, and in point of fact no essay does outdo *Of the Farm*.) I ended the letter by saying, "Now you don't need a philistine schmuck like me to tell you how good you are, but I assure you that not one sentence in the narrow miscellany of mine that Ms. Morris refers to would have been conceivable without your superb and unequallable flights of intellect, and that to mention you and me in the same breath is really a joke." To this embarrassing gush Murdoch wrote a prompt and gracious response: she said she hadn't seen the review anyway. I was pained, as all those who send raving letters to writers must be, by the failure of my praise of her to turn *me* somehow into a better person, and after a few days of rehearsing my shame to myself I pinpointed, while walking from one room to another, its real source. The awfulness of "Now you don't need a philistine schmuck like me . . ." had, it turned out, a direct recent antecedent: I had been, I now saw, patterning my letter on the example of a raucous, middle-aged, American woman character in Murdoch's own strange play *The Black Prince*. The character was straight-talking and used lots of words in the "schmuck" category, and (as Ms. Deborah Norton played her in late August 1989 at the Aldwych Theater in London) had an impressively loud, theatrical, braying laugh. In writing to Murdoch I felt uncomfortably American, and hence I over-played my Americanness in the letter *by using a tone taken directly from her own American character*. And I have made the same mistake with Updike in a number of places here. I fight the effrontery that my essayistic stance seems formally to call for, but because I invariably project Updike's self onto the heroes of his stories, I have to assign my *own* projected self the roles that remain—infuriating junior whis-tler, or bothersome golf-kid, or even, in the case of *Of the Farm*, the direct role of smart-aleck stepson. When I first read that novel in 1978, I found myself almost indifferent to the mental life of the narrator, and I instead matched myself to and felt jealous of the bright, eleven-year-old, science-fiction-reading child of his new wife. A decade later, the same confusion clearly persists, explaining my use of "Jeezamarooni" and my pretense of being a direct, enthu-siastic, slightly crazed, fringe, no-bullshit idiot savant who pipes up in opposition to Updike's peerless, polished, main-stream, genteel lucidity, when we all know perfectly well that it is not fair to call Updike genteel (I think a capsule reviewer in *7 Days* used that loaded word on him pretty recently): he is much too smart, too sneaky, too sexually appetitive, and too *mean* to fill that bill.

7

Mean? Yes, he is mean. He seems at times to admire meanness—I'm thinking, for instance, of that puzzling sentence
of his that always appears on Anne Tyler paperbacks: "Anne
Tyler is not merely good, she is *wickedly* good." He favors
the sudden devastating zingers that people spit at each other
in moments of anger. (In the scene that made me stop
reading *Marry Me*, the husband and wife really do spit, using
real saliva, at each other. [Actually the husband says "You
dumb cunt" and the wife then spits in his face.]) The mother
in *Of the Farm* hisses extraordinarily sharp things to Joey,
the divorced narrator, things like, "You can support one
woman, but not two," and "You've stolen my grandchildren
from me." (This second line, which like the first may not
exist, especially impressed my mother. In fact, I don't remember reading it myself; I only remember my mother once
citing it to me years ago as an instance of Updike's percep-
tiveness about divorce.) In *Marry Me*, again, he has the
protagonist swat one of his sons on the head in the middle

of dinner [really in the middle of saying grace], in a creak-
ingly psychological bit of "taking the divorce out on the
children." I hate this. In the carefully modulated dynamic
range of a psychological novel, a swat on the head or spit
in the face severs (and Murdoch's *A Severed Head* may well
be behind *Marry Me* and *Couples*) the bond with the reader
as unpleasantly as something out of a slasher movie. Maybe
it really happened—so much the worse for my opinion of
Updike. The meanness that first bothered me, though, when
I encountered it a decade ago, long before I was married,
was in a short story in *Pigeon Feathers* in which a young
husband returns with hamburgers and eats them happily
with his family in front of the fire, and thinks lovingly of
his wife's Joyceanly "smackwarm" thighs, and then, in the
next paragraph, says as narrator (the "you" directed at the
narrator's wife), "In the morning, to my relief, you are ugly.
. . . The skin between your breasts is a sad yellow." And a
little later, "Seven years have worn this woman." This hit
me as inexcusably brutal when I read it. I couldn't imagine
Updike's real, nonfictional wife reading that paragraph and
not being made very unhappy. You never know, though;
the internal mechanics of marriages are shielded from us,
and maybe in the months after that story came out the two
of them enjoyed a wry private joke whenever they went to
a party and she wore a dress with a high neckline and they
noticed some interlocutor's gaze drop to her breasts and

they saw together the little knowing look cross his unpleasantly salacious features as he thought to himself, Ho ho: high neckline to cover up all that canary-yellow, eh? Updike knows that people are going to assume that the fictional wife of an Updike-like male character corresponds closely with Updike's own real-life wife—after all, Updike himself angered Nabokov by suggesting that Ada was Vera. How can Updike have the whatever, the disempathy, I used re-frequently to ask myself, and ask myself right now, to put in print that his wife appeared ugly to him that morning, especially in so vivid a way? It just oughtn't to be done! It makes us readers imagine her speculating as she read it: "Which morning was he thinking that? He sat at the kitchen table eating breakfast and thinking I was ugly and worn! And I had no idea." It is not enough for Updike to say that he had to have the narrator be disapproving in the morning in order to protect him from the charge of "smackwarm" oversentimentality that the earlier passage invites (but does not deserve). When it's believable, sentiment is not a liability; nor would unnecessary cruelty on a subsequent page counterbalance true treacle. If Updike is doing this deliberately, in the belief that a high artistic intent sanctions it, it is just as bad as his doing it unknowingly, unaware that something like this might cause hurt.

The other example, more direct still, that I frequently think of in this connection is when Updike called Phaedra, the small press that brought out Nabokov's *The Eye* and *Nabokov's Quartet* (which included the supreme description of an Ithacan thaw, "part jewel, part mud," with the shadows from icicle-drops rising to meet the drops themselves and the "humble fluting" of the garbage cans), a "miserable little bindery." Such harshness is Nabokovian, of course (though Nabokov, protesting loudly, clearly didn't think so): Updike instanced Nabokov's "reflexive contempt" as one of the least attractive things about him (and man did I repeat that perfect adjective over to myself when I read it in a Berkeley library in 1981; I tried to use it in every sentence I uttered—"reflexive" acronyms, "reflexive" demonologies, "reflexive" car chases)—but Nabokov's hatreds were most of them directed at dead people: Freud, Dostoevski, Zola, etc. It is far more painful, I think, to see Phaedra called "a miserable little bindery" than to see Freud brushed off as a "Viennese quack." Think for a second of the employees of this firm (I don't know if it is still in business or not), proud to have lucked into publishing Nabokov and doing a perfectly acceptable job of it, too: think of them coming in to work the day after reading Updike's needlessly severe epitaph, hanging their heads. They should be praised and cheered on for playing an important part in Nabokov's publishing history, not held up to ridicule by a Jansonist Knopfer who thinks he is canny about bookmaking because he once worked a linotype machine and knows about widows and orphans. Foremost in my mind, as a matter of fact, as I wrote about the Franklin Library earlier in this essay, was my concern that I was on the verge of subjecting that publisher to the same sort of killing dismissal that Updike had dumped on Phaedra, and I toned down my words a little (though not enough), because, hey, why *do* that to people? Those who like the Franklin Library should be entitled to like the frigging Franklin Library—why should I cause them to look up at their shelf of monthly classics and suddenly feel doubtful? And those who work for the Franklin Library should be entitled to feel some pride in doing so. Think of the thousands of helpful dollars that the several Franklin combines—mint, porcelain, whatever—spend on magazine advertising: for that transfer of wealth alone they deserve our support. I do contend, though, that making fun of (not "poking fun at," please) the Franklin Library's binding and gilt is slightly more defensible than calling Phaedra miserable, since Phaedra was the only publisher of certain of Nabokov's books, whereas the sole reason for the Franklin Library's existence is to offer expensive, fancy versions of works that are for the most part available in other editions.

Fine. But would I know to go easy on the Franklin Library if Updike hadn't been so hard on Phaedra? He teaches even in his transgressions. Would I know to try always to forgive Updike's flaws if he hadn't treated his sometime hero, Nabokov, so peremptorily? In a review of *Despair*, Updike criticizes Nabokov for frittering away time on this sort of translation of early work when the world awaited another masterpiece [it's really a review of *Speak, Memory*: ". . . instead of composing the delightful, devilish, and unimaginable successor to *Pale Fire*, [he] fusses with backward-looking projects. . . ."]—and Updike's scolding seems woefully short on perception, considering that he had by then been in the business for at least fifteen years and was presumably well aware of the varieties of unhappiness (including reviewer-instigated unhappiness) and simple distraction or boredom or fatigue that can disrupt the rhythm of novel production, and especially considering that around 1961 he had himself gone through, as we now know from several hints here and there, such as in his introductory note to *Marry Me* [no, his introductory note to a story in Burnett's *This Is My Best*, reprinted in *Hugging the Shore*], a time of fear that he would never write again. (The sexual revolution disrupted and enriched the middle of Updike's writing career; the same might be said for the emigrations and gaps and second winds that the Bolshevik revolution imposed on Nabokov—but that is a sort of 80 percent rhetorical reviewery comparison that I never like reading; it is pleasant to do it, though, I must say.) And when *Ada* finally did arrive, Updike did such a number on it in his review that he felt compelled to explain in the introduction to *Picked-Up Pieces* that he writes faster than he reads (I'm not sure I understand what that gnomistry means, but I like it) and that therefore he may have grown impatient with some of the longer books he had to cover, such as *Ada*. Even the relatively good "cause for celebration" [no, "let us all rejoice"] review of *Glory* suddenly presents the charge that the book "never really awakens to its condition as a novel, its obligation to generate suspense." Can you imagine Nabokov soaking in his Geneva bathtub, squeezing a sponge of warm water over his head, an act he claimed (in that same *Tri-Quarterly* tribute) was one of the keenest pleasures of his later days, and then, as the water cooled on his face and the instant of dropleted bliss moved on, suddenly having the plug of his deserved happiness pulled by the memory of pipsqueak Updike's saying that all that work by himself and his translating son Dmitri fails to generate *suspense?* Updike is no master of cliff-hanging himself, remember. But at a certain point, I think, having gotten bad silly not-to-the-point reviews enough times yourself, you must finally think, I'll try it myself—I'll just *see what it is like* to charge someone with something idiotic like failing to offer suspense. Updike may have felt that it was a badge of veteran professionalism, of his status as a scarred and battle-seasoned dugong, to thump Nabokov once on the nose for suspenselessness. I can even almost imagine Updike hesitating a moment before typing "miserable little bindery" and then remembering, liberatingly, amorally, some particularly painful phrase that a reviewer had used on him, and his thinking "That dirty little fuckface! Well, I've taken my knocks! And *The Eye* is a poorly produced book and my job is to tell the truth—'miserable little bindery' it is!" But we see how cruelty begets cruelty: Nabokov's uncharitable streak took hold of Updike as he wrote about Nabokov; Updike's borrowed gall now infects me in my criticism of Updike.

Auden strikingly said (so I read in a review by Cyril Connolly in *The Evening Colonnade* and I'm paraphrasing and amplifying) that you should not speak ill of any writer, living or dead, to anyone but your closest friends, and absolutely not in print. Simply don't talk about, don't give space to, things you don't like. I think I agree with that, except in cases where the writer has invited criticism by being intemperately critical himself. Thus I was wrong to gripe about Updike's queasy adolescent heroes a little way back (there may be ex-queasy adolescents who like this quality in early Updike more than any other: why should I introduce an artificial dissatisfaction?), but I was justified in slamming him for slamming Nabokov as not supplying suspense or for calling his fictional wife yellow-skinned in the morning. We don't want the sum of pain or dissatisfaction to be increased by a writer's printed passage through the world. His task is simply to delight and to instruct as well as he can. I now think I see, in fact, that the contention that his fictive wife is matinally ugly and the contention that *Glory* fails to generate suspense grow out of one and the same infirmity in Updike's personality: he is able to discriminate between flaw and beauty too neatly in the things he loves. If you love, or at least like *Glory*, it cannot fail to do anything—and really, the only suspense a book needs, as Updike by now must know, having tolerantly motored through dozens of much more experimental bad novels for our benefit, is not "What will happen next?" but simply "Will I ever want to stop reading?" Likewise, if you love your wife, her yellow breast-skin can't make you jump so suddenly to the ascription of an industrial-strength predicate like "ugly." If on the other hand you dislike or are indifferent to an entity, then all sorts of elegantly shaded discriminations are possible.

From this distance, unable to check anything, with all of Updike's fiction packed away in boxes for the past year and a half, and most, if read, read years before that, I find that whenever I try to point out a flaw in his writing, I fail. For instance, all right, here is a real flaw—small but worthy of note. He gives each of his male characters a profession, and then he has him think in metaphors drawn from that profession. That's not right. In the beginning of a story called "The Day of the Dying Rabbit," a man, a photographer by trade, thinks of his baby as having f/2 eyes and skin like developing film. (Skin, not surprisingly considering Updike's debility, is all over the place in his fiction: the only example I can remember to substantiate this, though, aside from the yellowness above and the baby's skin here, is the case of the stepson in *Of the Farm*, who has, we learn, inherited his father's "sanguine and distant skin.") A photographer would not so directly use his professional equipment in the metaphors he applied to his immediate surroundings—he would use it *sometimes*, but not in the first paragraph of the story he told. Film and f-stops are huge real presences to him, and can't so easily be manipulated as tokens of comparison. Similarly, in *Of the Farm*, the narrator works in advertising [or "corporate image presentation"], and at one point he thinks, beautifully, while looking at a field, "*Flowers . . . the first advertisements.*" Not believable. Something different from this really happens to the metaphorically minded who are immersed in a particular specialized vocation. It is not that they resort to professional imagery when they want to describe something in daily life, such as their child or a field of flowers; it is rather that the specific equipment they use begins to absorb the rest of the world *into itself*—that in defending the advertising profession at a party, say, they will reach for an analogy to the bee-luring bloom, or when standing in the darkroom, with the film in their hands, they will think with surprise of how similar film is to their baby's skin. Their profession doesn't blanket the world; the world feeds its specifics into their profession. But Updike's only profession has been writing, whose basic equipment is the metaphor itself, and as a result he is less convincing on the direction of metaphorical flow for the white-collar worker than he might be. (The typewriter is his other tool: and notice that in *A Month of Sundays* he has a nice image of a typewriter ribbon winding itself back and forth ["A little fray in the typewriter ribbon moves back and forth like a sentry"], while he doesn't, I don't think, compare a scarf or mummy's windings or an Ace Bandage *to* a typewriter ribbon.) I am tempted for a moment to call this vocational metaphorizing habit of his a flaw—but do I really want "The Day of the Dying Rabbit" to begin any other way than as it does, with the f/2 eyes and the filmic skin? I do not, because its beautiful last sentence, as the expiring rabbit is compared to the sinking of photography paper in a trough of developer, depends entirely on it. A superb ending! And do I want the hero of *Of the Farm not* to think to himself, *Flowers, the first advertisements*? No, because without Updike's determination to get some measure of control over his constant instinct to fling outward with a simile by filtering his correspondences through the characters' offstage fictional professions, he would probably not have come up with this nice little thing, dropped as it is into the middle of a paragraph. My "No"s point, of course, to the defining quality of a major writer: he exists above the threshold of assent, that faint magenta line over which nothing he can do can possibly be felt as a mistake. Anything that causes doubt is either forgotten or is rerouted through some further circuit of forgiveness as more recalcitrant, and hence fresher, evidence of greatness. "I remember," says Henry James, of his first happy reading of Zola's *La Débâcle*, "that in the glow of my admiration there was not a reserve I had ever made that I was not ready to take back." That's the right attitude. It isn't, as Coleridge and other bardolators used to claim, that "not one word" of Shakespeare could be altered without destroying the whole—it is rather that these specific words were the ones Shakespeare happened to choose, and Shakespeare is a great man (though the plays are admittedly difficult to bear on television or on stage), and any particular clinker we might instance disappears into the general pension fund of admiration or becomes, if truly awful, merely interesting, revealing, never simply bad. In an oft-blurbed line, Updike once praised Nabokov for writing prose "the only way it should be written—that is, ecstatically": if true, this pronouncement ought to hold good for critical prose as well—and yet if I can force myself to utter a fixed doubt about Updike, it is paradoxically that he isn't ecstatic and immoderate enough about the writers he loves. He is too able to write a rave review that nonetheless includes the obligatory penultimate section of quibbles—his inability to blind himself to Nabokov's many weaknesses, in particular, and to see them as so much a part of Nabokov's foreordained self that they must be immediately explained away as part of the complex of traits that gave rise to all that is good in all those books, is the very weakness in Updike I have the most trouble forgiving. Books and life interpenetrate—like the drop of suntan oil on a page of Proust—and yet the measured, unsurprisable tone of many of Updike's book reviews is incompatible with the grief and turmoil and copulation in his novels. But he is a practicing professional critic, not a one-time closed book examiner as I am, and the duty of the practicing critic is to write about writers out of rhythm with his own passing inclinations and bursts of grateful affection—ecstasy and the assigned bound galleys only fall in perfect step on a few lucky occasions. Nor am I giving sufficient attention to the possibility that by publicly isolating a flaw in a writer he loves, Updike is simply trying to maintain his admiration against the inroads of second thoughts: like the Cat in the Hat scrubbing the bathtub, he offloads an awareness of the flaw onto the rest of us in an effort to restore his own appreciation to a higher state of purity. It may simply be, too, that he is not one of those writers who can gush without correcting himself a moment later: he notes with amused approval Nabokov's saying (of Joyce) something like "God can that man write!" [I haven't been able to find this]; but Updike may be better about failures and middling achievements—at seeing what good there is in the fundamentally not so hot. Or perhaps his prevailing coolness is conclusive proof of an enormous secret pride, of the deliberate inward reserve of a man intent on keeping his peculiarities intact over years of selling his literary opinions for money.

From this last vantage, I am the one making the big mistake, broadcasting my limitations, by proclaiming so *un*-reservedly that Updike is a genius. He doesn't want to hear me say that. How embarrassing! Nobody wants to hear that right now. But it is one of the telling traits of neotericks who think they have an outside shot at being called geniuses by later equally forward neotericks that they use the word "genius" as if it has a useful meaning. It doesn't. The word is like the gold confetti [no, "Silverdust"] that Updike's retail manager was using to make his holiday sign: it is a way of decorating a plain expression of enthusiasm with rarefied twinkly materials and tonalities. But I've been using it in this essay because sometimes we need a little twinkle. It disappoints me to see the label confined to obvious candidates like Flaubert or Henry James. Let's assume that right now, 1990, is as good as it gets. Let's try *genius* out on Updike!

Once in June of 1984 I was in the Paperback Booksmith (now Buddenbrooks) on Boylston Street when I picked up a novel by a man named Spackman, who was born in 1905 but was new on the horizon. It had an introduction by Edmund White, I think, whom I paid attention to despite my then homophobia because Nabokov had (so I dimly remembered from a blurb) praised him. I read a little of the introduction: Edmund White said that something in the tone of Spackman's essays seemed to have the authority of a person like Nabokov, "who knows he's a genius." It was an interesting idea, that Nabokov or Spackman or anyone else could *know*, in quite that definite way, so momentous a truth about himself. Did Edmund White say this of Nabokov because he, White, knew he was a genius himself, or because he knew he wasn't, or because he wasn't sure? The possibility of such knowledge made me uncomfortable, because of course I badly wanted to be a genius myself someday and I didn't yet feel any of that sort of foursquare certainty. But I did recognize the tone White meant: Yeats had it maybe, writers develop it over the years, an air of rangy assurance, built on the knowledge that there are plenty of people who are interested in what the guy has said up till now, and that the hush that has surrounded his past publications is unlikely to be replaced with indifference anytime soon, no matter what he does. This fixed certainty, the feeling of being pretty damned consequential, of tossing a few scraps to the eternally grateful who cluster around the podium, is in some personalities necessary perhaps to the completion of big, complex works. But is it true to say that Nabokov knew, in the sense of having a ground bass of belief that thrummed under everything he did, that he was a genius? He coveted the Nobel a tad too sincerely, I think, for him to be charged with such unwaveringness. (At least, an obituary I read in a Rochester paper said that his failure to receive the prize was one of the disappointments of his later years.) The unpleasant haughtiness of his late prefaces is, to this apologist, an indication of certainty and its morose opposite locked in struggle, as it is with Henry James's prefaces—even the megalomania of the twice-stroke-deluded and failing James dictating letters to family announcing his plans for fabulous renovations to his several imaginary Napoleonic palaces are sufficient proof to me that the decision to think of himself as a genius was an act of will, an imperial edict to himself, demanding constant fussy renewal and tending and plumping up to keep it from succumbing to doubt. Doubt, anxiousness, the nibbled lower lip, have to constitute the medium for most great works: Nabokov's emigration to the States and struggle to switch languages and make a living here, to the extent that it temporarily heightened the uncertainty of a constitutionally highly assured man, was what made possible *Pnin* and *Speak, Memory*, my two favorites. If, I thought, replacing Spackman on the shelf, Nabokov knew he was a genius back when he was writing *Glory* at age thirty, he knew it only intermittently: it was a fleeting suspicion, not certain knowledge, something incredibly exciting and jinxing and unthinkable that kept peeping at him over the rise of his best paragraphs, distinct from arrogance, mixed in with probably-nots and bright, leaping maybes. "Maybe I am, maybe I am!" And don't you have to admit, whatever your doubts are about the utility of the word, that it is pleasing, almost thrilling, to think of our very own living Updike at thirty-two or so writing "Her pointed yellow high-heeled shoes lay beside her feet as if dislodged by a sudden shift of momentum" and experiencing, when he looked at the words he had just so happily and casually combined, that same puzzled, curious, surprised sensation—"Maybe I am!"? I would be overdoing it to claim for so tender and closely observed and unassuming a domestic moment as this shot of his stockinged wife asleep that the passing shift of momentum it adduces is a distant transmuted aftershock of the enormous geophysical disaster of divorce;—that would be carrying it a bit too far, probably. But *something* big and refractive and vaguely frightening stole ripplingly through the living room that evening in the early sixties, and if it wasn't Divorce, then it had to be Genius.

I don't care so much whether from an encyclopedic perspective Updike is or isn't worthy of the word; what I want, tautologically if that's what it takes, is to determine to my own satisfaction that when he was just setting out, writing those early novels and stories, he was once in a while startled to catch himself in an idle moment tapping that golden finger at his own breastbone, because I need to know what someone who had plausibly reached such a conclusion about himself, however fleeting, could *do* with it, and did do with it, in a country and time I understood. Did the story "Leaves," of which he is justly proud (defending it against the charge that it was mere "lace-making," he said, "Well, if 'Leaves' is lace, it is taut and symmetrical lace, with scarce a loose thread"—and I liked this moment of sharp, slightly irritable confidence enough to remember it), come before or after such a detection, or was that very story first responsible for it? If through Updike I could learn at second hand what that brief, actuating intimation felt like, and nurse along any modest equivalencies in myself, if I could demonstrate to my strictest internal tribunals that I resembled Updike in certain important ways, then, thus inspired, I might just pivot myself one or two handholds higher along the sacred mimetic continuum. But the truth is that I am less like Updike than I used to think. We are both white, Eastern American, upper-middle-class, psoriatic, and heterosexual—but so what? That class includes millions. I feel closer to him than to any other living writer simply because I know more about him than any other living writer, but *he writes better than I do and he is smarter than I am* and that's what counts. This observation will surprise no one; it came, however, as quite a shock to me. Ten years ago, in my last semester of college, I was sitting in a dorm cafeteria at Bryn Mawr after lunch flipping through a library copy of *The Centaur* with my now-wife. We were pointing out passages we liked and ones we thought were no good. Work study students in white outfits were wiping off the tables all around us. "Now see, here he ruins it again!" I said, shaking my head. Scornfully I pointed to a sentence about gasoline shivering into an engine ["He poured shivering gasoline into the hungry motor"] and began criticizing Updike's habit of using words like "shivering" that were slightly too cutely anthropomorphizing for their contexts. (In the first Rabbit book there is, I seem to remember, a fair amount of skittering and slithering and whatnot, too, none of which I now mind . . . but *how strange*. I promised myself when I began this memory-dependent essay that I would not use the tempting phrase "seem to remember," which Updike uses once or twice in *Self-Consciousness*, and which appears on page 156 of *Speak, Memory* and a number of places in the late James, because Updike ought to be able to enjoy the satisfaction of having returned it single-handedly to currency for a year or two at least, and because "seem" is even on its own so treacherously alluring an Updikeanism, especially in the characteristic early uncoupled-copula rhythm of "her *blank* seemed, in its *blinkety blankness* and *blanketed blinkness,* almost *blonky* in the late afternoon *blonk*," that I always feel a twinge of derivativeness when I resort to it, even though Updike can hardly have a patent on something so wide-spread, and because anyway "seem to remember" has a mists-of-timey vagueness and veiledness that, so I thought two months ago, made it no good for me—but now look: it has offered itself to my typing fingertips, and they accepted!) After I delivered my criticism, I took note of my annoyed tone and suddenly wondered whether my now-wife was thinking to herself, What's he done that is so good that he thinks he can freely criticize Updike? So I asked her, "Do you think I'm a better writer than Updike?"

"I think you're smarter than he is, but that he's a better writer than you are," she said.

I nodded slowly, wounded, but pleased by her brave willingness, in the name of truth, to inflict such a wound and to muffle it so cleverly with a giant, distracting compliment. She thought I was smarter than Updike—I could live with that! Smarts, pure octane. I would go to the moon with them. But then, a month or two later, at home before starting my job, I was bothered by an identical doubt after reading some of *The Same Door*. Wasn't I a better writer than Updike had been at my age? I asked my mother.

There was a silence.

"But you *have* to think that!" I said. "I need you to think that."

"I think you will *be* a better writer than John Updike—I have every faith that you will be a better writer than John Updike."

That wasn't what I needed to know, though; the present

test was everything. I went off and lay on the floor near the loudspeakers for three minutes, in acute distress, letting the truth sink in. Then I went back to the kitchen and told my mother what my now-wife had said when I had asked her the same question.

"Well, yes!" my mother then said with evident relief. "Good for her. That's a good way to think of it."

And so I got several years of self-propulsion out of thinking that I was, if not a better writer, at least smarter than Updike. When my psoriasis turned inward, arthritizing first one knee and then a hip and ankle joint, I took this to be a manifestation of our difference: he had the surface involvement—style—while I had the deep-structural, immobilizing synovial ballooning of a superior mind. This psoriatic opposition still sometimes helps me to go on, but I am increasingly unsure what it means. It means something: despite all those claims (as in Trollope) that intelligence is a secondary trait in the novelist, I find I am much more liable to perk up when I hear that such and such a book has that particular quality than if lyricism, humor, compassion, atmosphere, period detail, etc., is claimed for it. No word so instantly reinforces my existing sympathies: I almost shouted with joy when I read someone quoted in a TLS a few years ago as saying, quite believably, that Proust was "the most intelligent person who ever wrote a novel." And I ordered Alan Hollinghurst's *The Swimming-Pool Library* entirely on the strength of another TLS review that ended by saying, "Few novels in recent years have been better written, and none I know of has been more intelligent." The novel is the greatest of all literary forms—the most adaptable and subspecialty-spanning and roomiest and most selfless, in the sense of not imposing artificialities on its practitioners and letting the pursuit of truth pull it forward—and as a result one recognizes the need to posit a certain variety of accompanying intelligence that is itself more adaptable, more multiplanar, sloppier, more impatient of formal designs, roomier, and more truth-drawn than other kinds, a variety that Proust, for instance, has a whole lot of. But what I have only slowly begun to see, over the past five years, is the dreadful degree of inefficiency and outright waste there is in the transmutation of this invisible and evasive, but real, intelligence into a piece of readable prose. You have to be at least twice as smart internally as you hope to be demonstrably in your writing. Therefore, in judging Updike's aptitudes that afternoon in the cafeteria, my now wife was undershooting their true magnitude by half. Updike is a better writer than I am *and* he is smarter than I am—not because intelligence has no meaning outside the written or spoken behavioral form it takes, but because all minds, dumb and smart alike, do such a poor job of impanating their doings in linear sentences.

Yet there is one specific point of similarity between Updike and me that is more important, from the point of view of my own novelistic ambition, than the others (class standing, geographical origin, race, etc.). Most good novelists have been women or homosexuals. The novel is *the* triumphant evolved creation, one increasingly has to think, of these two groups, who have cooperated more closely in this domain perhaps than in any other. This important truth couldn't hit us over the head until fairly recently: my own generation was the first to grow up with hard-core stars like Annette Haven a mere seventeen-year-old bike ride away, but more important, we were the first generation to grow up exposed to the range and subtlety and complexity of distinctively gay interests and ways of acting. These became common knowledge: they were no longer sexual semaphore among a gay elite, but were now a constant subject of discussion, delight, disgust, amusement, and enlightenment across an entire educated middle class. Our generation, I think it is fair to say, thinks it knows more about the *moeurs* of gaiety than any group so big and so mixed ever knew before, and armed with this marginally more sophisticated and less sniggering knowledge as we read past minorpieces and masterpieces, we gather hints and leap to conclusions with a confidence that would have horrified Edwardian bachelorettes. And slowly, with dawning amazement, as the results of our various informal surveys come in, we realize how staggeringly disproportionate our debt is to gaydom, in every possible area of literary deportment, but especially in the novel; and we mingle this knowledge with the long-recognized preeminence of women in the invention and perfection of the form, and we begin to get the uncomfortable sense, if we *aren't* gay or female, that we may have chosen a field we can't quite master. Heterosexual male novelists don't for the most part really *get it*, instinctively: they agree with Jane Austen that the novel is a magnificent thing, toward whose comprehension all other forms of writing, and indeed of art, aspire, and this big-time grandeur attracts them, but they find, much to their perplexity, that they can't internalize and refine upon its ways with quite the unstraining unconscious directness they displayed when thrashing happily through earlier intellectual challenges. At first they blame their false starts and archnesses on their own inexperience and continuing apprenticeship, and they redouble their efforts, but little by little they come to see, at first dispiritedly and then soon righteously, that they "stand outside the tradition"—that it is in a fundamental way alien to them. But they *are* smart, and ambitious, and hardworking, some of them, and they find that they can bleed off and redirect some of their other proficiencies in order artificially to bulk up the central novelistic understanding they want so badly and don't innately possess. They stretch the stretchiest of all forms so that it embraces what they do well. And finally they produce things that are, though great, oddities:

Ulysses, War and Peace, Pnin. In a field, then, in which heterosexuals end up so often on the periphery—as the legal counsel, drunken reviewers, imitative followers, codifiers, interpreters, academic apologists—for homosexual greatness, a person like Updike, who can be as *tarabiscoté* as George Saintsbury or Henry James, as foxily ironical as Lytton Strachey, as stylistically up to snuff as Pater, as metaphorically mother-witted as Proust, as zealously thematic as Melville, and who is thus in the same league at least with the bachelor-adepts of history, becomes supremely important to a writer like me, as a model of a man who has in his art successfully moved outside the limitations of his carnal circuitry.

I offer this line of argument tentatively, with every expectation that I will be laughed at for believing in so primitive a form of sexual determinism; it seems, however, unusually convincing to me at present because many of the novels that I've liked lately (*The Beautiful Room Is Empty, The Swimming-Pool Library, A Single Man*) have been so directly premised on gaiety: you feel their creators' exultation at having so much that wasn't sayable finally available for analysis, and you feel that the sudden unrestrained scope given to the truth-telling urge in the Eastern homosphere has lent energy and accuracy to these artists' nonsexual observations as well, as if they're thinking to themselves, Well fuck it, while I'm humming along at this level of candor, why should I propagate all the other received fastidiousnesses? Truths are jumping out at me from every direction! My overemphasis on sex is leading me back toward subtler revelations in the novel's traditional arena of social behavior, by jingo! (Have people talked, incidentally, about the prompting influence that Angus Wilson's *Hemlock and After* may have had on *Lolita*? Nabokov must have seen this gay book from 1952, in which the sole pure baddie is the heterosexual child molester, and thought that it was finally possible to amplify his reluctantly incinerated short story and show, now that gaiety was to an extent fictionally normalized, that even Humbert's unthinkable perversion was more complicated and remorse-filled than Angus Wilson had made it out to be. Nabokov must have noticed how the undisguisedly gay angle of attack lit the old, overnovelized mores from new angles, and that a similarly reawakened sense of nanomanners might result from a fictional situation whose raking unthinkableness stirred his own endocrines more.) Of course, Edmund White's apostrophe to the narrator's boyfriend's bottom (in a recent story in *Granta*) would not have been possible without Updike's wide-screen description of a neighbor's pussy; but nonetheless it is the homosexual novel right now, perhaps to an unusual degree, that seems to be driving us all toward advances and improvements.

8

"Also, homosexuals," my mother once very uncomfortably explained when I asked her what one was, after reading a Dear Abby column circa 1965, "often have unusually intense relationships with their mothers." That observation, which still seems quite true, used to worry me, until Updike's example slowly sank in, and I realized that straights could have strong maternal dependencies as well. My mother is very important to my writing life. She first told me, when I was still in grade school, and long before I had heard of Fitzgerald or Hemingway or Mailer, about a mysterious set of forces called "the enemies of promise" that brought writers low, especially in America; and when I finally read Cyril Connolly's book by that name, a few months after *The Atlantic* and *The New Yorker* accepted stories of mine in 1981, determined (in my expectation of instant celebrity) to be on guard against "the slimy mallows" of success and the "blue Bugloss" of journalism and the "nodding poppies" of indiscipline and chemical addiction and the rest of the besetting vocational dangers that it so winningly lists, I felt I was remembering a moral universe older and more primary than Aesop. Even these days, when I reread the 1960 Anchor paperback reissue, attractively subtitled "An Autobiography of Ideas," originally bought by my grandfather and now stained by a transparent liquid that seeped out the slackening mouth of a narrow pumpkin I had placed protectively on a stack of books in the window one Halloween when smashing was in vogue in the sixties and hadn't bothered to throw out for weeks (the hardbound of Cousteau's *World Without Sun* was also badly warped by the same Halloween syrup, and a fancily printed signed bibliography of Bernard Berenson was slightly foxed—and whenever I come across a book in my mother's bookcases that clearly evidences the part it played in supporting my one indoor pumpkin I feel a special thankfulness and affinity for it, as if the pile hadn't been random after all but prophetic of links and influences that in leaving their timed-release mark on me had allowed me to leave my vandalizing mark on them as well)—even now, rereading, I'm surprised to find that Connolly's funny, hung-over, peremptory, friendly style, and the scarily chronological lists of books he offers from the first third of this century (that is, the period of his own youth), and the battle he describes between the mandarins and the vernacular youmen ("Is there any hope? Is there a possibility of a new kind of prose developing out of a synthesis of Orlando and the

Tough Guy?"), and the occasional injections of his own life (like the plane tree in the sultry garden under which he begins the first chapter, and his description of himself as "a lazy, irresolute person, overvain and overmodest, unsure in my judgments and unable to finish what I have begun"), all affect me with an unexpectedly intense level of emotion. I wish I had known him. I wish he had written about Updike and Nabokov. I wish there weren't such things as older and younger generations and the inevitable deaths that make you think you have some special connection with a writer just because a pumpkin of yours once rotted on his book. I seem to think that if I don't turn out to be like Updike, who successfully feinted past every single enemy of promise there was (though the "charlock's shade," or sex—adultery in his case—did seem to give him some insomnia. . . . ah!— another link between Nabokov and Updike and Updike and me: insomnia!), then I will become a picturesque failure like Connolly. But no, I am even less like Connolly than I am like Updike: I'm not a drunk and in fact have a growing paranoia about liquor, I didn't have a string of successes in high school that rendered the rest of my life anticlimactic, and I haven't gotten sucked in to book reviewing. When fame and the other enemies do seek me out, though, and oddly enough they don't seem to be doing so yet, I will be fully prepared for their terrors, thanks to my mother and Cyril Connolly. Updike's mother, or rather her fictional equivalent in the story "Flight," tells him, as they stand on a hill overlooking their town, that everyone else is stuck there, but "You're going to fly"—and here perhaps is one of the more important differences (aside from writing talent and intelligence) between Updike and me: Updike's mother tells him what great things he's going to achieve, flying off to Harvard and *The Nuevo Yorker*, while mine simply assumed the great things and was already thinking ahead to their negative consequences. We didn't subscribe to either *The Atlantic* or *The New Yorker* when I was growing up; I read *Look, Life, Advertising Age, Car & Driver*, and *Popular Photography*. "Promise is guilt—promise is the capacity for letting other people down"—perhaps with these words from Connolly tolling in her memory, my mother, wanting me to have a good life and be a good person and not to fret too much about disappointing expectations, avoided hilltop predictions and other allusions to my promise, except that she told me more than once about a time in nursery school when I had drawn a picture of the three bears in which the trio weren't presented standing side by side in diminishing size, but were superimposed one in front of the other, indicating (to her) competencies in spatial manipulation beyond the nursery school level, and about another time that same nursery school year when I made a three-tiered organ keyboard by snipping three fringed lengths of paper and taping them together, each one layered over the next. "You were a special little kid," she said once. Why bother to pretend to be like Rabbit? ["Intellectually, I'm not essentially advanced over Harry Angstrom," Updike says in an interview.] He knew he was going to fly! And I knew I was a special little kid! We had great mothers! One way or another, we both knew we had promise! (Note the phonetic similarity of *The Enemies of Promise* and *The Anxiety of Influence*.) And Updike did then disappoint—not us, but his mother: he said somewhere that his mother still liked those early stories [or rather, his first *New Yorker* story] best of all the things he'd done; and I remember being struck by a passage in "Midpoint," a long autobiographical poem accompanied by deliberately indistinct pictures of Updike and his mother, in which she, or a motherish woman anyway, accuses him of writing about ugly things. ["you fed me tomatoes until I vomited / because you wanted me to grow and you / said my writing was 'a waste' about 'terrible people'."] Yet, in spite of his having let her down with some of his later work, which was unavoidable, he kept at it: and that is what is so magnificent about him as an example for the rest of us. He knows that some of his books are better than others, and he has even gone so far as to say (I first heard it on the 1983 PBS special about him, but I think the sentiment also appears in *Self-Consciousness*) that his best things, his ticket to immortality, are probably his early short stories; and yet, even knowing that, he has gone on writing. He quotes with approval a bracing sentence from Iris Murdoch, something about the writer moving on to write the next novel in order to make hasty amends for the last. He has brilliance and longevity.

But his mother, I learned just last week, is now dead. She died in October. My wife told me that there was a review of her last novel in *The New York Times Book Review* (January 14, 1990), which I can't read because they interviewed Updike in a sidebar, and I know if I turned to that page, I wouldn't be able to resist reading what Updike said about his mother, and then I would have again to apologize for not adhering to the principles of closed book examination. Plus I would be visited by highly unwelcome imaginings of what life will be like when (*if*, I still think) my own mother dies. I first heard Updike's voice in 1977 on a PBS radio show I turned on by chance—and what was he reading? He was reading a Mother's Day tribute to mothers before some national motherhood association. (*Where is this speech?* I haven't seen it in any of his collections.) I remember thinking, in surprise, Well, how very embarrassing for him! But over time I began to think of the speech as brave and ballsy. It was just as brave and ballsy for Proust to write about waiting for momma to come upstairs and tuck him in; but Proust's example simply couldn't have carried weight with me. Unless somebody like Updike (i.e., living and talented and heterosexual) had written about his mother, particularly in "Museums and Women" (one of my mother's favorite stories), I could not have written about mine—and, more to the point, I couldn't be writing about mine here. Without Updike's example I couldn't right now state how often over the past ten years my mother and I have talked about Updike—*long* Sunday-afternoon phone conversations between Boston and Rochester during which, after saying "I know we've already said this, but . . ." we covered once again one of our three main Updikean themes. These were, as my mother articulated them: (1) it was good for me to have to plug away at nonwriting jobs—Updike would have benefited from the same necessity; (2) Updike wrongly took sexual advantage of his irresistible prestige as a young writer to poach on suburban marriages while the husbands were off at work; and (3) my reluctance to go into all the bad things in my childhood—the parental fights over money, the dunners ringing the doorbell, the mess and the Saturday-morning fight about the *real* source of the mess, etc.—was admirable and kind of me but bad for my writing, because it severely limited my range: I should try, she said, to do more as Updike did by telling the bad and not worrying about the hurt this breach would cause. "Dad and Rache [my sister Rachel] and I will be very brave," she would say. And I would answer, "But there is nothing bad to tell! Some money squabbles—so what!"

Most important, without Updike's example I would not

be able to describe the first time I met the man himself, late in 1981, at the Xerox Auditorium in Rochester. He was in town giving a speech on Melville for the Friends of the Rochester Public Library. *I went with my mother.* (Even at this moment I am compelled to explain why a young man of twenty-four would be going to an event such as this with his mother—that I was back from some months spent in Berkeley with my now-wife, and that I was waiting for her to finish at Bryn Mawr and decide where she wanted to live so that I could follow her there.) I was feeling burstingly high-toned and unprovincial that evening, having been only a week or two earlier to the offices of *The New Yorker* for the first time, after announcing pretentiously to an editor (I had recently skimmed some of Evelyn Waugh's letters) that the telephone "made me nervous" and thus I *had* to go over my story with her in person. Because of my *New Yorker* trip, Updike's sudden appearance in my unprepossessing hometown took on to me the odd quality almost of a courtesy reciprocated. I remembered his account (somewhere) of E. B. White showing up on his doorstep and offering him a staff writing job, and I couldn't quite convince myself that his speech on Melville wasn't simply a pretext for covertly scoping out my upstate origins before giving the final OK to the high command to hire me. The whole audience seemed as jumpy and alert as I felt, much more eager than the concert-going audiences I was familiar with, as if we all thought that we were about to undergo a subtle but conclusive trial: what things we smiled shrewdly at and what angles we held our heads at, and whether we were capable of making it clear by our untroubled rumpledness and our audible head-scratching and our mock-impatient thumping of rolled programs on kneecaps that we were there purely out of sincere interest and not out of the cheapest, lowest lust for proximity, would mark us definitely as being worth the Oversoul's eternal attention or not.

Updike took the podium and began to read. We all, after *Self-Consciousness*, know to expect a stutter (he hadn't, however, in reading the motherhood address I heard on the radio); but to my prelapsarian ear it was so strangely contained and refined a faltering—a stately "pop, pop, pop" before a "p" word in an opening sentence ["popular"] like the three first bounces of a Ping-Pong ball before rapidity sets in—that I interpreted it more as a form of nonthesaural ornamentation than as a handicap; in fact, I first assumed there was simply something echoey wrong with the microphone or that in Updike's boredom with the idea of speechmaking he was pausing to blow thoughtful smoke rings. The popping happened no more than three times in the speech; maybe only twice. The last time I heard it I understood that it technically could be termed a stutter and I was amazed: Rochester, New York, of all places, was making Updike nervous. *I* was making him nervous.

That knowledge made me relax and listen to what he was saying a little more closely. He was trying to find out "what went wrong" with Melville's later novels. I don't know if he used those very words in the speech itself, but he had done so in an interview I'd read several months earlier called "Bech Interviews Me." Bech asks him at the end what he is up to now, and Updike answers (in *The New York Times Book Review*) "I've been reading the late Melville lately, to see what went wrong, if anything." For a writer to announce so casually in print ahead of time what he was reading and thinking about and working on, thereby coolly challenging all competitors to beat him to it and giving all detractors the time to elongate their yawns even further than normal, had struck me on that earlier Sunday as a highly impressive move; and there had been an admirable carelessness, too, in phrasing the chosen subject in such a way that the sneer-prone would be certain to apply it immediately to Updike's own career. We couldn't be sure whether he was playfully *pretending* to be struggling to profit by the example of Melville's untimely truncation, or whether he seriously believed himself to be, post-*Rabbit Is Rich*, at an analogous juncture. I still don't know. Standing miraculously in the downtown of my own city and treating the promised subject, he kept himself out of the argument entirely, avoiding contemporary references—only once did the audience, starved for dirt, go "Ooooh!" when Norman Mailer's name came up as an example of a writer who'd had a huge early success and had run into trouble getting beyond it. That high-schoolish "Ooooh!" from my Rochester—which, in its betrayed yearning to be privy to an imagined arena of high authorial spite, disgusted me—is the first thing I remember after the opening pops; probably I disliked it mostly because the rest of the audience had understood quicker than I had that Updike had said something that could be taken as a jibe. The third thing I remember is Updike's saying that one of Melville's books, perhaps *Billy Budd* [no, *The Confidence Man*], was "the most homosexual of Melville's works." And I hadn't even known Melville was gay! How stupid could I have been? In *bed* with Queequeg? I adjusted to this fact for a while, and began spooling out little theories about Conrad and Defoe, too (not only Friday—also the parrot: aural narcissism), and merchant shipping in general. He quoted a passage from *Pierre*, I think, to make the point that even in a book with a completely landlocked subject matter [no, *Clarel*, a poem about the Holy Land], Melville's oceangoing mind irrepressibly reached for sea similes in describing what it saw. But the best moment by far was when Updike figured out how much Melville was paid, in current dollars, for his writing, and used that low figure to make the cheering point that the United States was not then, as it happily is now, populous and literate enough to sustain a writer even of Melville's difficulty. ["The United States of his time would seem to have been like Third World countries today—able to breed a literary community of sorts but with a reading public insufficiently large to sustain a free-lance writer of books."]

It was a smooth speech . . . but "smooth" sounds patronizing. It dissatisfied me then because it wasn't fiendish enough—it didn't take one of Melville's sentences or images and do a mad-scientist number on it, brandishing the analytical instruments while they still steamed from their autoclaves, exulting in every banned or questionable area of forensics, clutching and rattling the chosen page with a seizure of louped scrutiny that alone could make the drowned man's words rise again. But now I think I see better that equanimity is as much a critical virtue as mania is; what disappoints me about the speech today, when I think over it, is simply that it was too much Melville and not enough Updike. All it had of Updike was that stylized stutter. But Roland Collins, then chairman of the University of Rochester's English Department, who had invited Updike, raved afterward to my mother and me: "When I heard it was going to be on Melville, I thought 'Oh Lord no,' but it was really *extremely* good."

"It was, it was," we agreed; and I suspect that if I were to reread it now (which I can just barely keep from doing: *Hugging the Shore*, where it is collected along with an essay on Hawthorne I also have never read, is in a pile of books somewhere in this very room, glowing around the clock with the capacity to disprove my arguments and demonstrate my inaccuracies once I open it; and I have even ordered *Assorted Prose*, the omnibus from Updike's first writing decade, with its reviews of Kierkegaard and Tillich, and its funny introductory sentence about the time, early on, when Updike had been in danger of becoming viewed as *The New Yorker*'s resident expert in philosophical and theological speculation, so that whenever one of the "slim, worthy-looking volumes" by Tillich or Heidegger crossed the book review editor's desk, it zoomed straight to him—or is that all in *Picked-Up Pieces?* [it is]—so that when I need to correct my misquotations it will be here to refer to as well: I want desperately to be *done* with this study!), if I were to reread it now I would admire it more than I did then, because I can appreciate now how hard it is to stay at that ideal benevolent altitude, from which vantage each book is the size of a county, its highways and townships and eyesores and terrain easily discernible, and the farseeing reader can take in at a glance, as an instance of a general type, an image or incident that would have entoiled me for three months.

There was a small table to one side of the auditorium, near the stage; Updike took a seat there and began signing books. A line grew up the middle aisle that my mother and I finally took our place in; it moved surprisingly fast. The woman ahead of us held an armload of perhaps fifteen books, most paperbacks: when she reached the table where Updike sat she handed them over in bundles of four or five. He politely signed them all and nodded a thanks to her. Then it was our turn. Smiling fatuously, I handed him a brand-new copy of *Rabbit Is Rich* I had bought that day. This act was the outcome of some serious thought. I had wondered whether I should have him sign anything at all, since the practice was so nutty—complete strangers wanting a man to scribble in their book, body and blood, all of that. (Oh, but it's all worth it, because Updike is repayingly brilliant in *Self-Consciousness* when he mentions a strange interruption in his act of signature between the "p" and the "d" of his last name that has increased, not decreased, in severity after all these years of book-signing—this cursive hiccup he neatly links with the stutter. [No—surprisingly, he does *not* make that link, in "On Being a Self Forever."]) Wouldn't it be, I reflected, more of a statement of my understanding of what his life was like if I consciously didn't take up his time by meeting him and having his book signed? Years later, I could say, when I finally did meet him, "I saw you in Rochester, but I thought better of having you sign my copy of your book." No, I had to meet him that day. As a compromise I entertained the notion of bringing some relatively uncommon book of his in to sign; but for it to impress him it would have had to have been very special: not merely *The Carpentered Hen* (which I didn't own anyway) or that early paperback of *Of the Farm*, with its Van Heusen shirt man pensively embracing a "Christina's World" woman, but something really *unusual*, like the mysterious edition of chapter one of *Marry Me* published by some press with a name like Abandocali or Adobacondi or Abacondai. [It's Albondocani.] I've never seen this version, by the way; I've wondered, though, over the years, whenever I looked at *Marry Me*'s copyright page and saw it cited there, what his motives were in making that limited edition—was it a gift, and if so, given the dune-time tryst it lovingly details, *to whom?* Copyright pages are, if I may wander from the scene at the Xerox Auditorium for a further moment for Harold Bloom's benefit, at the molten center of the neophyte's anxiety of influence: especially their ritualistic, commaed-off phrase "in somewhat different form." "Portions of this book first appeared, in somewhat different form, in [magazine]." "The following stories first appeared, in somewhat [or 'slightly'] different form, in [magazine]." Am I right in thinking that my generation is madly plagiarizing Updike when we all publish books with this classic example of the Updikean rhythm murmuring its parentage in our copyright pages? Even if he simply took it over from some predecessor, it has come to stand completely for Updike's prosody. For my first novel I was taking no chances: I took a look at the copyright page of *The Centaur* and copied it. For my second novel, though, I was determined to strike out on my own in this area. The word "portions" had come to seem (like "home" instead of "house") decisively non-U, in the snobbish Mitfordian sense, and I decided to try the more U word "parts." After much erasure and galley rethinking, the passage on my copyright page now reads: "Chapter 1 and *parts* of chapters 3 and 4 first appeared in *The New Yorker*. A brief passage in chapter 9 first appeared, *in different form*, in *The Atlantic*" (italics mine). [At least, so it reads in the UK edition (Granta/Penguin), which was published first. A week before printing, the American publisher, Grove Weidenfeld, completely reworded the first sentence without telling me, *reinstating* the "portions" that I'd been so careful to avoid.] I meant to convey volumes by that dropping of "somewhat" between "in" and "different" in *The Atlantic*'s acknowledgment: I meant to indicate that I had done a major overhaul of that 1984 passage; I meant to make it clear that I had improved as a writer since then—although I'm not in fact sure it *is* better in its second version: rewritings, even tiny changes (e.g., Walter "Palm," James's mannered revisitings, Nabokov's embaubling of *Conclusive Evidence* as collated for us by Updike in an interesting review) are always dangerous; but improvement or not it had to be different for me to interest myself in it enough to work it in. Don DeLillo went even further in the copyright page of his first novel, about football: he said "in *very* different form" (italics mine), which I used unfoundedly to take to mean that he'd gotten pissed off by the degree of editorial intervention at *The New Yorker* and employed that "very" of the final version as his tiny revenge. [None of this is true, oddly enough: *End Zone* is not DeLillo's first novel, and there is nothing like the "in very different form" that I remembered reading in the acknowledgment. What is wrong with me?] (Of the two dreams I've had about Updike, one contains a prominent copyright page. It occurred at 5:30 in the morning on May 31, 1986. I pulled a hardcover version of *The Same Door* off some staff writer's bookshelf. I turned at once to the copyright page and saw

Copyright © 1954, 1955, 1956, 1934 by John Updike

I had known that looking at the book would make me unhappy, but when I noticed the last date I felt a momentary mean-spirited triumph, thinking that poor young Updike hadn't even been able to keep a typo out of his copyright page—as I had felt in real life once earlier, when I had discovered Iris Murdoch listed as "Murdock" in the index to *Picked-Up Pieces*. But then I looked again, and the "34" blurred and re-formed itself as "39," which I believed was the year that Updike was twenty-eight, and I let the book spine slump into my hand so that the book closed; the moment it closed I closed my eyes and felt a sob reach my face, because always, always, Updike turned out to be right in the end. Then I woke. In the second dream, which occurred at 2:20 in the morning on September 23, 1986, Updike showed up drunk, fedora askew, in New Orleans and had to work his way back to New York as a train conductor. I worried about him, quite surprised that he was that much of a drinker, but also impressed by his ability to bluff his way into being a train conductor, and I wondered if the ability was acquired from all those years of novel-writing, or was simply the result of a natural capacity to charm. He had said somewhere, I remembered in the dream, that there was a little bit of a salesman in the writer, which made him able to do things like make public appearances and sign books. [What he really said was: "I don't dislike the spouting-off, the conjuring-up of opinions. That's show biz, and you don't go into this business without a touch of ham. But as a practitioner trying to keep practicing in an age of publicity, I can only decry the drain on the brain," etc.])

I finally decided, anyway, that I shouldn't try to be fancy that evening: I wanted to meet him and my only chance was going to be if I had a book for him to sign and it should simply be a brand-new copy of his latest, *Rabbit Is Rich*. I handed it to him and he bent his head to the task. I watched his pen form the word "John"—it looked more like "Jon"— and I said to his extraordinarily full head of hair: "I was at *The New Yorker* offices last week—I noticed you had a story scheduled for very soon!"

"Yes." He blinked. And then very politely, knowing that it was what I wanted him to do, he asked, "And what were you doing at *The New Yorker*?"

"I have a story coming out pretty soon, too. So we're fellow contributors."

"And what's your name?"

I told him.

"And what issue is it?"

I told him.

"Good," he said.

"And I'm his mother!" said my mother, waving. (Why didn't I do the proper thing and introduce her?)

Updike nodded at us both. "I look forward to reading it," he said, giving us back his novel. My mother and I smiled good-bye and walked away, with flushed, What-new-fields-can-we-conquer-now? faces. "Well!" my mother said. "Wow! That was a lot of fun! Was that all right do you think?"

"Yeah, it was good, I think," I said.

Behind us, Updike went on signing, signing.

When I told the story of this meeting to my wife a year ago, she slid down in her chair with her hands over her face in mortification. "I would never have done it," she said. "But you're different from me."

9

I would never have done it either—drag in *The New Yorker* name so obviously to get his attention—except that *life was too short* not to. Those ticking seconds of signature might be the only chance I would ever get to embarrass myself in his presence. When the excessively shy force themselves to be forward, they are frequently surprisingly unsubtle and overdirect and even rude: they have entered an extreme region beyond their normal personality, an area of social crime where gradations don't count; unavailable to them are the instincts and taboos that booming extroverts, who know the territory of self-advancement far better, can rely on. The same goes for constitutionally ungross people who push themselves to chime in with something off-color—in choosing to go along they step into a world so saturated with revulsions that its esthetic structure is impossible for them to discern, and as a result they shout out some horrible inopportune conversation-stopper, often relying on a word like "pustulating," when natural Rabelaisians—who afterward exchange knowing glances with each other that say, "Sad—*way* out of his league"—know to keep their colostomy sacks under wraps for the moment. Which referenced sacks bring us to the second time I met Updike—for I did, as it happened, get a further opportunity to embarrass myself.

At the offices of the *Harvard Lampoon*, in November 1984, I sprang out in front of him near a plate of ham cuttings as he was hurrying to leave the post-Harvard-Yale-game party. A friend (insofar as male friendship is possible) said I should come with him to this party because the building was worth seeing. As he showed me around, sensing my testy inner readiness to see the Lampoon's flaws and its self-satisfaction, he bad-mouthed the institution severely—nobody really good except Updike came through here, he said, gesturing at the second-floor library, where all the Benchleys and more recent wizards were shelved. It was true that the idea of working on a college magazine would have been inconceivable to me at Haverford. (Well, no—in fact I once submitted two poems to the literary magazine, which were rejected.) Why waste weeks working on something that is distributed internally, that doesn't appear on a transcript; something that doesn't count? It's like putting on plays for your family; it's grade-school stuff. But clearly the *Harvard Lampoon* did count in New York: Updike himself said once (I think) that a *New Yorker* editor had noticed something of his, light verse perhaps, in the *Lampoon* and had written asking to see more. And he had done the introduction to an anthology of *Lampoon* humor—he obviously thought of it as something worth thinking about even after he had graduated. Yet his physical presence that day was, to me at least, completely unexpected. *Did he come every time the game was in Cambridge?* Had he actually *been* to the Harvard-Yale game that day? God I hoped not. It was very important to me that this postgame Lampoon visit was not typical Updike behavior—I wanted him not to have anything to do with writers' conferences, literary awards committees, college reunions, magazine anniversaries, idiotic flag-waving school spirit: his only allegiances should be, I think I thought, a Craigenputtock purist myself by force of my own obscurity and isolation, to the isolated writers he liked: Henry Green, Nabokov, Tyler, Proust, Murdoch, Melville. And yet if he hadn't felt enough fondness for his old school magazine to show up that day, I wouldn't have had my chance to wait for him near the ham tidbits, steeling myself to be pushy. I knew it was pointless, but I wanted to talk to him more than anyone else I didn't know. I spied on him as he stood in a rearward room, giving serious advice to an exceedingly tall person who was editor or president of the Lampoon that year. Then he took his leave of everyone and briskly walked along the long neomedieval table of hewn food toward the door. He was done socializing; I could see that. But I sprang out anyway. I blocked his path, standing with my hand held out for him to shake. Yes, the editor/president with whom he had been in close conference was very tall and skinny; but *I* was very tall and skinny too—perhaps taller, skinnier! I needed my outsider's moment!

"Hi, I'm Nick Baker."

"I'm John Updike."

"I know." (This "I know" is a faint source of shame to me now, but it is nonetheless what I said.) "We met once in Rochester, but very briefly."

He nodded, still thinking he could escape by giving the general appearance of hurry. But I wasn't going to let him go. "I, um, had a story in *The New Yorker* a long time ago."

Resigned to this standard interchange ("people who want something from me" is one of the categories of humanity he lists in "Getting the Words Out" as not inspiring him to stutter), he asked me what the story was about. I told him, and he said, "Mmm," but he didn't look as if he remembered. He asked me my name again. I told him and mentioned the long story I had had in *The Atlantic*, too. Closing his eyes, pressing on his forehead with his index and thumb, he forced himself to recall who I was. "Didn't you also write a story about some musicians on the West Coast?" he suddenly asked.

Surprising as this may sound, I had to think for a second. It was a work I didn't want to exist. Both *The Atlantic* and

The New Yorker had rejected it, as had many little magazines; it had finally appeared in a place called, emblematically, *The Little Magazine*, where John Gardner had seen it and included it in the 1982 volume of *Best American Short Stories* that he edited before he was killed on his motorcycle, too soon for me to get around to writing him a thank-you. In his introduction Gardner called it "very slight" (he also called it "beautiful," but naturally I paid no attention to that); he almost apologized for including it over other more "major" entries. That soured me on it—I didn't want to be a lightweight. But the main reason I had tried to forget about the story was that it was, by a hair, my first published work, appearing a week or two before the story in *The New Yorker*, and I was extremely sensitive then to the fateful progression in which (see Updike, Helprin, Gill, and the others) a writer has his first story published in *The New Yorker* and lifts off from there into a string of successes. When *The Little Magazine* came in the mail on that November day in 1981, incontrovertibly first, it was an evil portent: in a stroke it condemned me as a late bloomer, a come-from-behind guy. Now when I collected my stories in a book (if I ever published more stories, which by 1984, when I stood in the Lampoon building, was looking doubtful, since I wasn't writing much of anything by then and the *The New Yorker* and *The Atlantic* had rejected or bought and shelved the few pieces of fiction I had sent out), I would either have to leave out the *Little Magazine* story entirely, or I would have to *begin* the book with it, since, in another case of copyright-page anxiety, I was determined to do just as Updike had done [on the copyright pages of *The Same Door* and *The Music School*] in proclaiming that "They [the stories] were written in the order they have here." I had more or less decided to leave the story out. The extreme childishness of my attitude is obvious to me now, because once you've published a book your dignity's dependence on magazines temporarily disappears, but back then the columbarium-like array of quarterlies, displayed on angled steel shelves or in piles on tables or in echoing alphabetization in places like the University of Rochester's periodical reading room, subscribed to and renewed when necessary and stamped with the date received and warehoused and eventually sent to the bindery and put on other, more inaccessible shelves whose lighting system was often controlled by little oven-timers you had to turn and whose insistent grinding rushed you to your next call number, threatened me with annihilation. All those arbitrarily evocative names (once, under the influence of poetic titling habits, pop groups gave themselves and their vanity corporations and their albums colorful concrete noun-names, but at some point the balance shifted and little magazine titles began to seem instead derivative of pop practices), and all the regional awards, all the calls for manuscripts in the classifieds of *Coda* (now *Poets and Writers*), all that awful, awful young writing like mine that should never have been published, and the contributors blazoned on the covers as if they were big-drawing names when they were utter unknowns like me, and the general conviction that most of the publications were, even more so than the *Harvard Lampoon*, places that just didn't count, weren't read, had no reason for being, made me determined to keep my indiscriminate distance from all of them. So when Updike finally remembered who I was on the strength of that *Little Magazine* story I was taken aback—I didn't know for an instant what he was talking about. "Musicians on the West Coast?" I said, puzzled, and then, realizing that I probably appeared to him to be pretending to have to make an effort to remember something that I really knew right off the bat, I said, "Yes! Right! I did!"

"A lovely thing," said Updike. He also praised something else of mine that appeared in *The Atlantic*. And *he said that I should keep writing because I had a gift*. Should I not be including this pronouncement here? Is it self-serving? No, because mainly it shows Updike to be civil and generous in person, which is a thing worth knowing, and because it could easily be nothing more than the "mere babble of politeness," as Henry James called some of his letters, and because my patently self-serving inclusion of it shows me to be even less likable than I might possibly otherwise have seemed. (Who will sort out the self-servingness of self-effacement?) Anyway, how can I not retain Updike's moment of encouragement, when it is one of the very few *events* I have to offer in this whole plasmodium? It isn't as if Updike said, "Nick *Baker!* Holy moly! Congratulations on being you! You're going to *fly!*" It isn't as if what he said was anything like what Schumann said about Brahms. Still, "a lovely thing" was a lovely thing for him to say—it helped me; it altered my opinion about that story, which I now will certainly include if I ever put out a book of stories. But did it also, I now discover myself wondering—and even my suggestion of such a possibility should serve as a warning to all eminent and tolerant writers not to be nice to people who pounce on them at parties—did it also lower him ever so slightly, in the old Groucho Marxian manner, in my estimation, since I can see, rereading the story now, that it is replete with false touches? Why didn't he see through it? I wonder; in seeing through it myself I suspect for a minute that I have found a blind spot in him to the kind of cheapness it exhibits—when really he was simply doing what he knew I wanted him to do, which was to recognize my existence as a writer, to bless me by remembering who I was.

He asked me how I made a living, and I told him. "When I first got out of college . . ." I started to say.

"College *here?*" he interrupted, raising his eyebrows as if to settle an important question, and pointing at the floor.

"Myeah," I said. A lie! A pathetic lie! Again he had caught

me off guard; I knew he was in a rush and I had only a minute left to talk to him and in the instant of decision I shied at explaining that I was just someone's guest and wasn't aware of the Lampoon's tradition of secrecy and that I'd really gone to Haverford College and had been rejected by Harvard's grad school in philosophy and hadn't applied as an undergraduate to Harvard because I had read Frank Conroy's *Stop Time*, in which the hero ends up debarking from the Paoli Local at Haverford, and because several relatives had gone to Haverford, and because my mother had gone to Bryn Mawr, and because I was scared that Harvard would reject me as a transfer student from Eastman anyway. Rather than explain this, or rather than simply saying "No, I'm a guest," which would have sufficed, I in effect told the classic, inexcusable, singles-bar kind of lie by letting John Updike think I'd gone to Harvard. He looked at me sharply for a second, as if he knew I was lying. (My capsule bio in the back of *Best American Short Stories 1982* said "Haverford.") I went on talking about my employment history. He said his son was thinking of taking a teaching job, but he, Updike, wasn't sure it was such a good idea. "It's hard," he said, meaning hard to make a living at writing.

"It is hard," I said. "But when I get deflated I go back to one of your early stories and I'm all fired up again!"

He had been backing away by then, knowing the obligatory praise-heaping and groveling scene was coming; at this he shook his head and waved and walked out. Had I insulted him by saying "early stories"? I had meant it as an allusion to his own statement on the PBS show that his early stories had the best chance of surviving; and I meant that I went back to them in particular because they were stories written when he was my age. (In 1984 I was twenty-seven.) But what I didn't understand then was that he might not want his assessment of his work taken at face value. Do I, when I say that my *Little Magazine* story is "cheap," necessarily want people to agree wholeheartedly with me? Not at all. I don't want them to disagree strenuously to my face, either—I'm not fishing in quite that naked sense—but I do want to imagine that there are people out there thinking to themselves as they read that Oh no! I don't find that story cheap at all! Perhaps there should be a corollary of Auden's rule—the one about keeping your negative opinions about writers to yourself—that you must never bad-mouth your own past productions, since any good elements in them (and there *are* a few OK things in my first published story) are harmed in the overspill of your general dismissal. Look at what happens after you read Pynchon's *Slow Learner* introduction to his early stories—he talks about how doubtful he is about them, how he looked up things in old Baedekers and did anything he could to be impressively obscure, and as you read it you think, How appealingly modest of the guy to tell us this, but after a few years go by, what he said takes on altogether too much authority—his virtuous self-criticism has hurt your capacity to appreciate residual merit. In later life, as I remember, Joyce thought that *Portrait of the Artist as a Young Man* was his best book; as a result I may never finish *Ulysses*. And Updike's high ranking of his early stories may well have made it too easy for me, less inclined to read his novels anyway, to excuse myself from making the slight additional effort in that direction, when there are surely plenty of rewards to be had.

I had a pimple or two on my forehead that day at the Harvard Lampoon. (Synalar, a topical steroid I was using to treat my psoriasis, often flipflopped my forehead skin toward the other, oilier extreme.) When *Roger's Version* came out a year or two later [1986], with its nice pale blue cover faintly inset with crosses, I stood in Lauriat's in downtown Boston and read the first few pages. My single powerful reaction was: *I was Dale.* Updike was describing me. I actually believed (and still do believe, though with less conviction) that Updike got Dale's extreme gawky tallness, his thinning hair, his bad skin, his overeager, technotalkative, slack-but-smart way of speaking, and Roger's own immediate sense of being threatened by and mildly disliking Dale, all from that one tiny encounter with me. Updike had broken free from my chatlock, I figured, gone home muttering to himself about pushy younger writers, gotten up the next morning, and written me into the first scene of his novel as a computer nerd. A few years later I mentioned this theory to my mother, who had just read the book, as I still have not. She didn't like the notion at all. "You, the model for that awful Dale? No."

Imagine how difficult it is for me to keep from searching out her copy of *Roger's Version* right now (she loaned it to us) and reading those first pages over again to be sure that Updike really does mention Dale's bad skin and his height—that I haven't just wished the parallel into being. [Dale is "the type of young man I like least: tall, much taller than I, and pale with an indoors passion. His waxy pallor was touched along the underside of his jaw with acne. . . . His dirty-looking, somewhat curly brown hair, I could see at his temples, was already beginning to thin."] But even when the critical quarantine is lifted, I probably will read *Of the Farm* again before I read straight through *Roger's Version*. I resist the books for which Updike did lots of impressive research, such as *Roger's Version* or *The Coup*—and when last year I read, on the back of the paperback of Patrick Süskind's *Perfume*, Updike's (just) praise of it as "beautifully researched," irritable jealousy made me oppose this sort of preparatory effort more firmly than ever, though I did not hesitate to pop into the library myself under any pretext. The follow-up novel to Süskind's *Perfume, The Pigeon*, came out right around the time excerpts from my first novel were appearing: in a review of it Updike spoke in general terms about writers who resort to magnification in an effort to find events and objects that haven't already been described to death. I was fairly sure, here again, that he was referring obliquely to me. The question of whether he would come out with a more direct review of my own book as well (he would have had to do so outside *The New Yorker*, since "portions" of it had appeared there, and in recent years he had rarely reviewed outside)—a judicious, unsurprised, encouraging review—was the subject of prayer and dread quite often in my insomnias of late 1987, while I wrote it; which period marked, indeed, the very peak of my Updike "obsession."

He said that he wrote *The Poorhouse Fair* in six months, so I quit my job and gave myself that same stretch to finish my first book. As I wrote it I read, more or less in this order, some of the journals of the Goncourt brothers for the first time, some of *Flaubert's Parrot* for the first time, some of Huysmans's *Against the Grain* for the first time, some of Chapman's *William Lloyd Garrison* for the first time, all of Edmund Gosse's *Father and Son* for the first time, all of Roth's *My Life as a Man* for the first time, some of Nabokov's *Glory* for the twentieth time, half of Exley's *A Fan's Notes* for the first time, some of *The Collected Prose* of Elizabeth Bishop for the first time, some of Edna O'Brien's *Night* for the first time, and I reread a little of Isherwood's *Mr. Norris Changes Trains*. But none of these, not even *Glory*, felt close enough to me. Finally I took down *Of the Farm*: it was short, as my novel was turning out to be, and I already knew how good it was. (In 1989 Updike praised Mulisch's *The Assault* as a "short, perfect novel." Yes, the description applies to *Of the Farm*, too—if perfection can allow for those secondary circuits of forgiveness mentioned earlier—but secretly I regretted that Updike had used up this nice phrase on Mulisch, before I came out with a book that he could lay it on. And yet if he ever were to say something like that about me, the praise would become enemy number one of promise.) I went through *Of the Farm* very slowly that fall, a few pages every morning before I took up with my own manuscript. It was the first time since 1978 that I had read one of Updike's books uninterruptedly from cover to cover, without skipping around or putting it aside before reaching the end. I let it soak in. I figured out how many words it had and compared that figure with my chapter subtotals. It became the measure of all worth. More than once I yelled "He's a fucking maestro!" More than once I had tears in my eyes. For instance, I cried at the aforementioned description of the raindrops on the window screen like a crossword puzzle or a "sampler half-stitched": it killed for the time being a patch of screen description of my own, but that didn't matter, because Updike's paragraph was so fine that my competitiveness went away; and when I found that Elizabeth Bishop's 1948 *New Yorker* story called "The Housekeeper" also had a screen whose clinging raindrops "fill[ed] the squares with cross-stitch effects that came and went," this parallel only demonstrated to me how much more Updike could do with the same piece of reality: he had lifted it from the status of incidental setting and made its qualities part of the moral power and permanency of his mother's house—no, I will say further, in a typical bit of appreciative overheatedness, that this screen *is* the novel itself—that geometric, formal, conventional, antimalarial grid through which you look into Daumier's Third Class Carriage of social life (the reference here is strainingly obscure: I just mean that Daumier's painting is overlaid with, because it's unfinished, I guess, a matrix of vertical and horizontal lines—but now I worry, does Updike talk about Daumier in his brand-new *Just Looking*?), but which as you continue to write distracts you with its interesting nearby droplets and tiny rips and odorous rust dust and habit of shaking slightly in winds, until the "young embroiderer of the canvas of life," as Henry James says in a cognate passage in the preface to *Roderick Hudson* that I've just been reading,

soon beg[ins] to work in terror, fairly, of the vast expanse of that surface, of the boundless number of its distinct perforations for the needle, and of the tendency inherent in his many-coloured flowers and figures to cover and consume as many as possible of the little holes.

What I liked so much about *Of the Farm* was that Updike's terror was under control; the proportion between consumed and unconsumed holes was just right; you could still *see through* the mesh of the screen, but the clinging metaphorical figures, such as the droplet-needlework image itself, were there in cross-eyed, painstaking abundance.

Unfortunately, I finished reading *Of the Farm* a few weeks before I finished writing my book; looking around for more Updike to prolong the helpful high, I read the awards-acceptance speeches he includes in *Hugging the Shore*. As a result, I lay awake two nights planning the acceptance speech I would make when my novel won the National Book Award. There were two problems relating to the speech. First, Updike had set a standard of felicitous gratitude that I could never better. Should I be in reaction somber, or incoherently at a loss, or shy-debutantishly brief? Should I apologize for all the bad places in my book—even supply some last-minute textual corrections to the lorgnetted assembly? "And on page sixty eight, if you will indulge me in one more amendment, six lines up from the bottom, the word 'twiddle' should properly read 'fiddle.'" Should I thank Updike for inspiring me? Should I say right out how hard it was to write an acceptance speech after reading the Castiglionean models he provided in *Hugging the Shore*? I simply could not formulate a first sentence that felt interesting and properly heterogenous and yet acceptably free from Updike's influence. The second problem was, assuming I did come up with a speech that did the job, and I delivered it without incident, and years went by—what should I *do* with the text then? Updike was right to include his in a prose book—acceptance speeches were a distinct form of literature, akin to toasts and letters but with their own distinct requirements and opportunities—but doing so was somewhat unusual, was it not, was itself a part of Updike's originality? If I included my speech I would feel that I was slavishly copying Updike, more so even than in the matter of the copyright-page acknowledgment. On the other hand, I didn't want to deliver a speech that I didn't think was worth publishing permanently. And I liked very much the idea that Updike could look at *Picked-Up Pieces* or *Hugging the Shore* and know that they contained all of his nonfictional self from that particular decade. Yet it might be a nice idea, attractively humble, to have a bunch of miscellaneous writings of acceptable quality left over for the posthumous mop-up volume. Or no—the arrogance of engineering your appearance of humility was itself fluorescently vile. The only thing to do was to refuse to accept the award altogether. But that extreme would merely be a ripoff of Pasternak and Sartre, both Nobel-decliners.

Lucky for me, I didn't win anyway. I wasn't one of the five nominees. In fact, my publisher didn't even bother to send in my book for consideration. I won no awards of any

kind—not the NBA, the PEN/Faulkner, the PEN/Heming-
way, the Whiting Foundation, the Joe Savago New Voice
Award, the National Book Critics Circle, or a Big Mac. Not
a single dinky award! Fuck them all! But no, it's good, it's
good, it's better that way: few people will imitate me, because there is clearly no glory in it, and my relatively un-
recognized and unfêted position allows me, just barely, to
write this kind of a nose-pressed-against-the-store-window
book, if book it turns out to be, about Updike. I did get
some very good reviews—but the interesting thing about
those bolts of elation was that though Updike was in my
thoughts constantly while I wrote my book, not a single
reviewer mentioned him as a possible antecedent. I was
reminiscent of, owed much to, or failed to measure up to
Abish, Barth, Borges, Bove, Calvino, Friedman, Joyce, Lem,
O'Brien (Flann, not Tim or Edna), Perec, Ponge, Proust,
Robbe-Grillet, Sterne, Tati, and Trow—never Updike.
What can this mean? That I think I'm influenced when I'm
not? Or that there are differences between a role-model sort
of influence and a purely stylistic one? [Updike's name did
come up in a few reviews of my second novel, but by then
I had said that he and Nabokov were heroes in several
interviews.]

I *felt* myself to be stylistically influenced—deeply so. Even
in the matter of skin I was his plagiaristic follower: a short
time after I finished the book, finally joining the ranks of

novelists, my psoriasis got suddenly much worse. It covered my entire buttock region, as Day-Glo-colored as a baboon's, and most of my legs, much of my back, my neck, my arms. My navel was a disaster. I Vaselined myself like a Channel swimmer. I did not want to be touched or seen. There were grease stains and blood spots on all my pants and on all the pillowcases—my ears bled. I had to wipe off the receivers of pay phones on my shirttail after I used them. And truly no man has ever itched like I itched—it was a hyper-itch, a deep, swarming sort of interior toothpick sculpture, a sub-cutaneous "blooming buzzing confusion." I had bloody skin under my fingernails from compulsive scratching that I cleaned out as I read by drawing the corner of a ten-page chunk of *Of the Farm* or *Hugging the Shore* under the rim of the nail and brushing the pink profligacy away. I put off the trip to the dermatologist that I knew was imminent, though, because I wanted to see whether my disease had it in itself to be worse, more consuming, than Updike's dis-ease—not only in the structural arthritic symptoms, which I had learned to live with, but right on the surface. Whose prose cells divided more uncontrollably? Whose canvas of visible self was more erythematously elaborated? I wanted to reach that mystical moment he describes, when "I couldn't turn my head without pain." And I did reach it. One after-noon I stood naked in the middle of my study with my arms extended and realized that I did not want to walk, sit down, dress, read, think, or live. I was becoming a giant lesion. I went to the doctor. He offered me the choice of going to Mass General or Beth Israel for phototherapy; I chose Beth Israel, because it was slightly closer, but as I was driving home I groaned, because I remembered that Updike had written that he went to Mass General: I might have sprung out at him again as he showed up for a treatment, wearing the prescribed pair of comically zooty, wraparound, retinally protective NoIr sunglasses. But I thought no, by this time (1988) he surely had bought his own home PUVA booth for thirty thousand, avoiding the long drive and unpleasant interaction with other people's skin flakes that mark these visits. I loved going, though, at least for the first year: since quitting my job I had no professional obligations, no jotted meetings in a time management system, no schedule of any kind, and my thrice-a-week irradiations were a welcome bit of external bustle. By the time I moved away from Boston and bought *Self-Consciousness*, where the psoriasis essay appears in revised form, Updike had pulled ahead of me again: he had switched to the grandmaster drug methotrexate, the liver-witherer, while I hung fire with PUVA; so that even if I had chosen Mass General, I realized, I never would have run into him and become his friend and swapped repellent plaque-tectonic anecdotes at the Harvard Gardens on Cambridge St. and finally reached that inconceivable eventuality when, inspired by phototherapy's clubby locker-room atmosphere of goggles, towels, sunscreen ointments, and hasty dressing, he might have asked, "Do you golf?"

But that's all right. I don't need to be his psoriatic friend and fellow sufferer. I have, in at least one tiny and characteristically dermal instance, communicated with him in a permanent way. I'm not referring to my half-nuts theories that I am Dale in *Roger's Version* or that he is really talking about me in a book review of *The Pigeon*. In that 1981 story about musicians on the West Coast that he told me he liked, I wrote:

> The first violinist . . . began inspecting his left index finger, pressing it tenderly with his right thumb.
> "How's your callus doing?" the cellist asked.
> "Professor Belanyi said to file it down, so I just took a nail file and zapped the hard part off." He extended the finger. There was a yellowish area on the end that had been flattened by a file. "It hurts when I start playing, then then the skin warms up and it gets flexible."
> The cellist said, "You know that Miriam's callus on her middle finger split once just before a concert, and she had to play the whole Lalo concerto with a Band-Aid on?"

In Updike's 1984 novel, *The Witches of Eastwick*, in a passage that I can finally look up and quote exactly, because my book is nearly done, Darryl praises Jane's cello playing:

> "You have precision. . . . Without precision, *beaucoup de rien*, huh? Even your thumb, on your thumb position: you really keep that pressure on, where a lot of

men crump out, it hurts too much." He pulled her left
hand closer to his face and caressed the side of her
thumb. "See that?" he said to Alexandra, brandishing
Jane's hand as if it were detached, a dead thing to be
admired. "That is one beautiful callus."

Laughably tiny, you say? Hard to credit? Maybe. Still, I
suspect that Updike would not have written about Jane's
beautiful cello-callus unless I had first written about a mu-
sical callus that I had once seen and touched in Southern
California. Because I exist in print, Updike's book is, I think,
ever so slightly different. For a minute or two, sometime in
1983, the direction of indebtedness was reversed. *I* have influenced *him*. And that's all the imaginary friendship I need.

For further information about Granta Books
and a full list of titles, please write to us at

Granta Books

2/3 HANOVER YARD

NOEL ROAD

LONDON

N1 8BE

enclosing a stamped, addressed envelope

_____

You can visit our website at

http://www.granta.com